2−

THE HARD ROAD TO KLONDIKE

*Sean O hEocfhaidh
took down this story.
Proinnsias O Conluain edited it
for publication in Irish;
to both of them the translator
offers this English version.*

THE HARD ROAD
TO KLONDIKE

MICHEAL MacGOWAN

TRANSLATED FROM IRISH BY
VALENTIN IREMONGER

The Collins Press

This edition published in 2003 by
The Collins Press,
West Link Park,
Doughcloyne,
Wilton,
Cork

First Published in 1962 by Routledge and Kegan Paul Ltd.

British Library Cataloguing in Publication data.

Printed in Ireland by Colourbooks Ltd.

ISBN: 1-903464-35-8

Contents

Preface

It was more or less by accident that the story in this book came to be written down. In 1941, I started to collect folklore in Cloghaneely for the Irish Folklore Commission. It was at the height of the war and thousands of tons of shipping were being sunk by day and night just out from us beyond Tory Island. But it's an ill wind that blows nobody any good—the market for cattle was booming.

On the sixth of April, the fair was being held at Gortahork. I was staying with Sean McSweeney whose house was by the fair-green and I was using the fair as a means of getting to know people. I was standing on the doorstep when I noticed a sturdy old man across from me who was having some trouble getting his pipe going. He lifted his head and, probably because he knew me by sight, he came over and spoke to me.

'My heart is broken with this old pipe,' he said. 'You, now, move about a lot and you should be able to tell me where I'd get a good one.'

'I can do that,' I said, 'and it's not all that far away.'

I had just bought a new pipe that I hadn't smoked at all. I went back into the house, got the pipe and handed it to him. He liked it and thanked me for it fervently.

That's how I got to know Micky MacGowan; and I suppose it was the same pipe that gave another twist to my life. In the autumn of 1943, I married Anna MacGowan, Micky's daughter. I went to live in his house and was able to get to know him properly.

He was a strong sturdy man who must have been about five feet nine inches high when young. Sinewy and robust, he was also intelligent and quick-witted. His mind, indeed, was as tough as his broad chest and his character was such that he was remembered well, no matter where he went. He spoke forthrightly and wouldn't hide what he thought from any person; high or low were all the same to him: he had no soothering tongue. He was truthful and upright—so truthful that he expected everybody to be like himself. By nature, he was a little bit abrupt, even fiery (as can be seen from his story) but that may have come from the way he had spent a good portion of his life. In the places where he had been, it was every man for himself. Anyone who couldn't look after himself, as Micky said, 'got it in the neck'.

His faith was very strong. He was one of those people who knew that it was not by chance or without purpose that he had been born into the world. He always tried hard to carry out the obligations of his beliefs.

All his life, he had a great interest in his native tongue. He disliked those who reneged their birthright and particularly those who went from their home and after a while came back with their accents 'polished up'. His proudest moments were when he had a crowd of Irish speakers around him while, talking to them, he tried to increase their vocabulary. He both amused and helped me in this way. In the summer, when the visitors would come and stand looking at the sea-serpent's rib over the front gate, he used to go down and talk to them; and very dissatisfied he'd be with anyone who didn't know Irish. 'Be damned but you're a funny crowd,' he'd say, 'not knowing a word of your own language'—and this, as like as not, to visiting Englishmen!

Micky and myself spent many a night beside the fire talking and yarning—and he was a first-class story-teller. As usual with his like, he'd speak frequently about the ways of the world and about the changes he'd seen in his time. And so would come the stories and the events of his life. It cheered him up, at the end of his days as he sat snugly by the fire, to tell stories that would set your skin tingling and your heart beating faster. Not that any of his household paid any attention to him: they had heard it all before and often; but I had a great liking for him and, as this was living lore which the story-teller himself had actually experienced, I thought it worth saving and storing in the archives of the Folklore Commission. I also had the idea that some social historian would be interested in it in days to come.

I listened carefully to the whole story. I made notes of all the different adventures; and when I had that done, I asked Micky one night if he would record all that he had told me. He averred that he would and welcome; so when I had got some semblance of order into my notes, he started off. I didn't try to tax him beyond his resources at any time but bit by bit I got the whole story from him. The tale could be as long again but I think that what we have here is sufficient to give the reader an idea of the lives our people led trying to keep body and soul together and at the same time send home the odd few pennies to those who were still there holding the fort, so to speak.

As I took down the story, I never thought that one day it would be published. But a couple of years ago, my friend Proinsias O Conluain came our way looking for folklore about St. Patrick's Day for a programme on Radio Eireann. I told him the story of how Micky and his friends spent the Feast in Klondike and, in the course of our conversation, I mentioned that I had a copy of Micky's own account of it. Proinsias abstracted enough from the manuscripts for a series of programmes; but he didn't stop there. He worked away until he had edited the whole story and shaped it into a book; he gave me no rest or respite until he had the material ready to be submitted for the Oireachtas Literary Competitions in 1958 where it won the annual Award of the Irish Book Club.

'The pen's trace remains though the hand that held it dies,' as the old saying has it, and so it has been with Micky. He died on the 29th November, 1948. Without knowing it, he left his monument behind him. May he have eternal rest.

SEAN O hEOCHAIDH

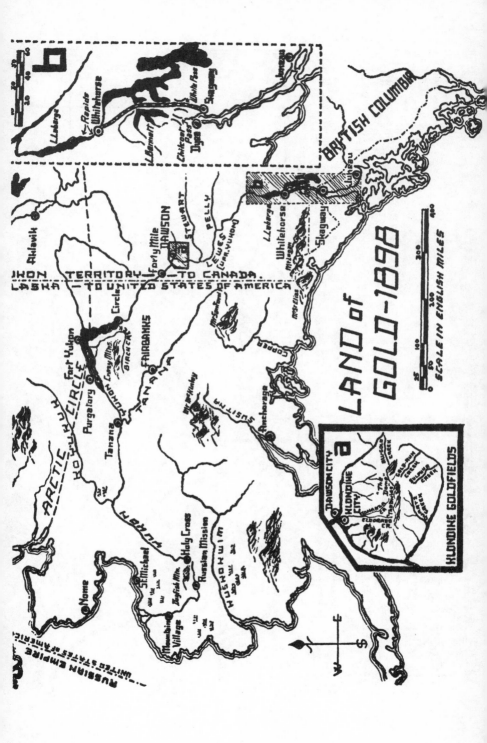

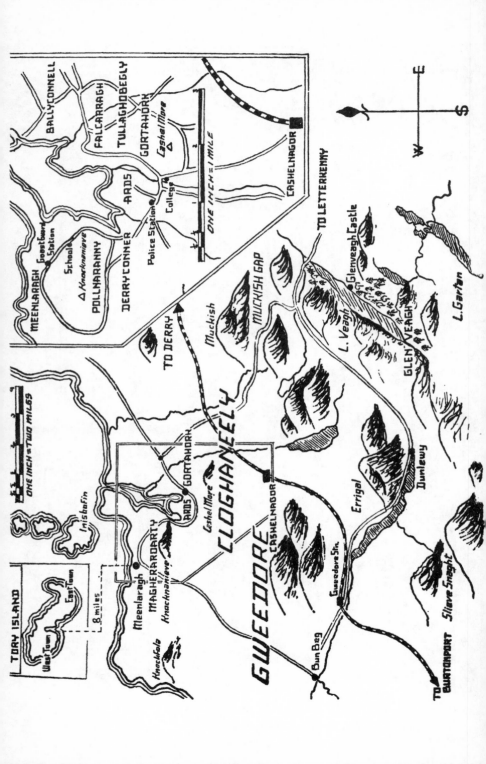

A Cabin in Cloghaneely

AT THE FOOT OF CROCKNANEEVE

Anyone who spends a while at Gortahork in County Donegal is bound to hear about Crocknaneeve, the noble hill that rises in the western part of Cloghaneely between the village and the setting sun. It's not without reason that it's known as Crocknaneeve. It is said that St. Columbkille, St. Finan and St. Begley went to the top of the hill one day and, of course, there lay the whole parish spread out below them. What they intended to do was to divide the parish between them and, as Tory was a large important area then, each of them wanted to get the island for himself. What they had arranged was that each man would go wherever his little cross fell.

St. Begley flung his cross first and said: 'My little cross will go to Tory with the help of God.' But instead the cross turned eastwards and fell in the place that's called Tullaghobegley even now.

St. Finan threw his little cross then and said the same thing: 'My little cross will go to Tory with the help of God.' The cross didn't go to Tory but hit the crag out east at the edge of the sea at the place called St. Finan's Waterfall to this day. When the saint went east to where the cross had fallen, he blessed the water and devout people still go on pilgrimage there.

St. Columbkille then flung his little cross and what he said was: 'With the help of God, my little cross will go to Tory.' St. Columbkille asked the help of God first and that's why his cross reached the island.

The seas opened before the saint then, so the old story goes, and he walked to Tory.

At the foot of Crocknaneeve is the townland of Derryconor and the far portion of it lies by the sea and is called Pollanaranny. It is there, in a little thatched cottage that still stands, I came into the world on the 22nd November, 1865. My father was Thomas MacGowan and my mother Bridget Cannon. Twelve children all told were in our household of which I was the eldest, a position that left me open to enough anguish all throughout my life.

It's not easy for this generation to understand the circumstances of life as they were when I was young. Often now, as I think back over life as it was then, I feel as if I'm dreaming. Life was untroubled enough in the manner of the times and the people were content even if they didn't think so then. Neither turmoil nor tumult, on sea or on land, existed to disturb them. Neither books nor papers were available to them; they were unlearnt and untaught and they were never troubled by any convulsions in the great world outside. If they had to go from home they went on foot but that didn't give them a day's worry. Hardly more than two people in the whole parish had a clock, and if they had to look to being punctual—which was seldom—they relied on the sun or on the moon. To make a long story short, it was little they had to do with the world outside except for the news that a travelling man would bring them from time to time.

But there was another side to the story. The people of this area—including my own people—were as poor as could be. They had no land worth talking about and it was hard to make any kind of a living out of the little bits of soil between the rocks. But there was one gift the people had: there was friendship and charity among them; they helped one another in work and in trouble, in adversity and in pain and it was that neighbourliness which, with the grace of God, was the solid stanchion of their lives.

There was no work to be had by the men of my parish in the district when I was young—apart from the bit they'd do on their own parcel of land and, God knows, that wouldn't keep food in their mouths for long. Mostly they survived on potatoes and they worked hard to raise that particular crop. Spades were used in our area all the time. There was an odd wooden plough here and there but there were so many rocks and stones around the place that even that could hardly be used. There was no talk then about artificial fertilisers and, as every family had only one cow, that left natural manure in short supply. People had to go down to the sea-shore to watch the tides early and late, collecting sea-weed and wrack to put on the land. Even this needed permission from the landlord and then something, small or large, would be added to the rent for this privilege. Anyone who couldn't pay this would have to spend so many days working on the landlord's estate at Ballyconnell. In a good year, the crop would be fine but in a bad year, when it failed, both beast and human would go hungry.

When I was young, there were households that ate potatoes four times a day—on two occasions they were boiled, and on the other two they were in the form of potato-cakes. They lay heavy on the stomach but, in those days, fresh fish were as plentiful as grass—and as cheap. Fresh ling and cod from Tory sold at twopence apiece. They had these and other good food as well: limpets, periwinkles, cockles, dulse, laver, mussels. Many is the time when there would be real hardship that they would have to make do with that food alone. I often heard the old people say it was this food saved the people in the 'Bad Year' (1847) and in another poor year when I was a child.

All the houses in the area were thatched. Most of them had three rooms: a kitchen and two bedrooms. Usually the kitchen was in the middle with a room on either side. Our house was like that. The byres used to be against the house at that time also and, indeed, I remember seeing cows tied in some of the kitchens. Reeds were used to thatch our house and the other houses in the area. They were plentiful down by the sand-banks at Magheraroarty and everyone's land had a strip by the sea

3

both there and at Derryconor. They have such to this day. The bogs and their limits are the same now as they were hundreds of years ago. This is the way the limits are fixed: as the reeds are cut, those along the edge are left uncut so that the owner can come along and tie what remains into knots. This is done year after year and in this way everyone knows his own. When the men were cutting reeds as I was young they had a kind of toothed sickle—a sickle with an edge something like a saw. The reeds had to be cut under the sand and they would go about the cutting on soft days when there would be nothing much doing on the land. They would often be wet to the skin at this work. Then they would sell a load of reeds for a couple of shillings and well might it be said that this was money earned the hard way.

FEVER

Because of the byres being against the houses when I was young, the dung-heaps were always near by the doors. It was customary at times to dig a hole in the ground near the door to put the dung in. As the summer grew hotter, of course, this became extremely unhealthy and few were the years when this practice did not give rise to sickness and especially fevers.

My mother, God be with her, was a midwife. Doctors weren't too plentiful in those days and there were no nurses, nor signs of them, for many a long year afterwards; but these talented women were here and there round the neighbourhood and anyone who needed them had only to call them.

One year, when I was a strong enough youngster, one of these fevers struck the homesteads. It laid our own neighbours low and, as was usual at that time, nothing would satisfy my mother but to go and see if there was anything she could do for them. She didn't know what was wrong with them but, the poor creature, it wasn't long until she found out. We were, as I have said, twelve strong in children and my mother got little rest. When she came back from the neighbour's house, she went on with her work as usual but next day a couple of the household went down sick and by the second day there was no one under the roof that wasn't laid low except my mother herself. My father and the whole lot of the children were struck by the worst form of the fever.

Many a father and mother were left heartbroken by the same fever. My own mother was left there without anybody at all to help her but in those days there were women here and there in the countryside knowledgeable about curing fevers and it was customary for them to come and help those who had no one to look after them. My mother heard of one of these that at the time was back in the Rosses and she sent word for her to come over. She came straight away and gave my mother every help while we were on the flat of our backs. I don't remember now what her right name was but, any time my mother spoke about her afterwards, Peggy Mor of the Rosses was what she called her. My mother and the lot of us were certainly under a great obligation to her.

It was a good summer that year with a killing stuffy heat that was hard enough on people in their full health not to speak of those in the throes of a fever. Our house, like the others in the district, was small and narrow and, since the windows couldn't be opened (being built in one piece into the wall), we had to leave the doors wide open to the whole of Ireland throughout the night. Only a couple of us could fit on a bed and, as there was such a tribe in the house, some of us had to shake down on straw in the kitchen and sleep there. We lay a long time incapable with the women waiting on us; but I may say that there was only the one thing that did us any good while we were sick and that was potheen. A lot of it was being made at that time in the parish of Cloghaneely—the best of the juice of the barley. The habit of it was woven into the life of the people. Memories of it are so tied up with my own youth and particularly with that fever that I must give some kind of an account about it.

POTHEEN

My own people were making potheen just the same as everybody else. Not to put a tooth in it, they were somewhat astray because of it. They had neither a day's peace nor a night's rest on account it and it sent enough of them such a way that they hardly knew what they were doing. At times, they'd drink so much of it that they'd go off their heads altogether. Others in the neighbourhood were just the same. They'd forget about their little bits of land and often enough drag themselve᷾ and their families down into misfortune and poverty. There weren't many to keep an eye open for the potheen-makers in those days other than the crowd we used to call the 'Watermen'* in Magheraroarty and there weren't enough of them to keep up with the 'industry'. Normally, the 'Watermen' didn't carry any firearms or weapons other than bayonets and, God knows, more murderous instruments you never came across. Anyway, they never carried guns whenever I saw them out after the potheen.

Near enough to the houses, the potheen was made. There wasn't a rivulet or stream in the place that hadn't a still-house beside it. A good-sized stream with the best of water in it flows down between our house and Magheraroarty. Down by the main road, there's a sizeable fall in the stream and, at the foot of this fall, my own people had a fine still-house. There's a nice secluded little dell in that place and, if you didn't know it was there, you'd never find it.

Many is the time I was told, when I was a young lad, to take food down to those who were working in the dell. There were a few men down there one day running a drop and myself and another lad were sent down with a bite of food to them. We reached the place easily enough and when we got to the 'hide-out' everything was going ahead fine. We were hardly over the threshold when, what do you think, two of the 'Watermen' were hard on our heels. Whether they had been watching and following us, or whether they had seen the smoke rising from the still-house, I cannot say, but they came straight after us and nearly caught all who were inside. Some of the Magheraroarty men who were at home saw the 'Watermen' on the trail and followed them, screeching at the top of their voices, to the bank of the stream away across from where we were. When the men working at the still heard the commotion and uproar, up and away with them, leaving the two of us who were only children behind them. They were afraid of

*Water-bailiffs.

being captured themselves but they knew that nothing would happen to us.

The 'Watermen' came right into the still-house and, while they were inside breaking up and wrecking the equipment, we faced towards home. We made for the stream—towards the place where there was a lot of large rocks that made a kind of causeway over it. By myself, I could have jumped over the stream to the other side but my companion couldn't so I stayed on one of the stones trying to give him a helping hand. The stones were slippery enough and there was a good strong flow in the stream and, if we fell into the large pool that was beside us, there is little doubt but that we'd be drowned.

The men on the other side of the stream gathered and started to throw stones in an effort to reach the still-house where the 'Watermen' were; and, between them and the screeching and roaring of myself and my companion, I tell you there were rows and ructions going on for some time. But the 'Watermen' were better soldiers than those pitching the stones; they came out and urged the crowd across to come and help us over the stream before we were drowned. There was one man there, Seamus Johnny, and he plucked up enough courage to come across to us and help us over. When the men had us out of the way, then the battle started in earnest. They all crossed over the stream and the stone-throwing and the murder knew no bounds, being carried on over the ditches and sometimes on the main road. It was getting late in the evening and as the pursuit of the 'Watermen' drew towards Ards Point, the number of people following them was growing. Indeed, they followed them for about a mile and a half along the main road.

A MAN IS KILLED

As the sun was setting, a poor old man named Patrick Mor was walking down the main road after spending a day in the bog cutting turf. He heard the hubbub and the roaring nearing him and he didn't know from God what was wrong or what was the cause of it. There was a large rock overhanging the roadway and he thought he would shelter under it until all the trouble had gone past. When the first of the 'Watermen' came to the place where the old man was hiding, he saw him and thought that it was somebody lying in ambush for him. And what do you think, didn't he go straight up to him and run his bayonet through his heart, killing him stone dead on the spot!

After killing this poor old man, the 'Waterman' ran as fast as he could and made for the first house he could see along the road. And what house was it but the house of the man he had just killed! He went in and hastily closed and bolted the door behind himself. There was no one there save the woman of the house and an old woman who was getting a night's lodging from her. By then, of course, nobody could either go in or out. When the men who were throwing the stones came to the overhanging rock where Patrick Mor had taken shelter, they saw his body lying beside the road, his heart's blood flowing and he stretched stone dead there. One of them went straight away for the priest and the others went to get a shutter and bring him home.

When they reached the house, the murderer was inside with the door locked and he refused to let them in. They were planning to set the house on fire over his head and one of them was already up on the thatch with a match in his hand when the priest arrived. The priest made it clear that he would not allow such a thing to be done. 'When you didn't do that,' he said, 'before I came, you're not going to do it now while I have the Blessed Sacrament with me.' They listened to what the priest said and they didn't fire the house at all. While this was going on, the police came. The 'Waterman' inside opened the door for them and they took him away. Nobody touched him then. He was safe enough with the police.

Shortly after this, the law began to close in rightly on the potheen-makers. The 'Watermen' knew some of the men that took part in the chase and they did their level best to have them sent to prison but they never succeeded in getting enough evidence against them. It wasn't them that should have been put in prison, at all events, but the man who did the murder, but he always had the excuse that while the others were stoning him, he was defending himself. I needn't say that they had the law all their own way at that time and he got away with it.

He didn't come to much good afterwards, by all accounts, as we heard that, when he left Magheraroarty, he took his own life.

MY FATHER IN PRISON

That's one of the dangers I came through safely when I was young because of the potheen. All the things that took place as a result of it left a heavy mark on the district and on my own people in particular. One of the effects of the business was that both the police and the 'Watermen' were after the potheen from then on with an implacable resolve to catch up with those responsible for making it. It wasn't long afterwards that we were all laid out with the fever and, I needn't tell you that there wasn't a better cure than a drop of the hard stuff. The spirits that carried the law's blessing were both scarce and dear and there was no talk of apothecaries' remedies then. I don't remember rightly now whether a drop of potheen had been made by my father or whether one of the neighbours brought it in to my mother but, whatever the cause, there was a drop in the house and my mother would give us a spoonful now and again to help us. Our house, I may mention, was built just by the road-side and the police were going up and down past it very frequently in their search for the potheen. They knew that nearly everybody in the house was laid low with the fever and it was easy for them to throw a look in at us. It was a suffocating period and, when there'd be a bit of a fire down, my mother couldn't close over the door and all she would do at night-time would be to put a creel or two in the doorway. Air and coolness were what those who were lying around on the floor wanted.

One night that the police were going by on the road, they must have seen my mother giving us a spoonful of the potheen. After a while, in comes a pair of them, up between the beds and to and fro where we lay on the mats, nosing around until they reached the room beyond and searched it. That didn't do them much good. Back with them and what do you think didn't they find the bottle in the gable and take it with them. It was all the two poor old women, my mother and Peggy Mor, had to keep

9

their hearts up in themselves and in us. The police left them without a thing and they were in a bad way.

Two of us didn't rise out of the fever at all—two of the girls. It was well over a year before the last of the ten of us that were left got safely over the sickness and none of us was very much good for a long time afterwards. We were all wasted, thin and weak and just about barely able to stand on our feet. My father was the worst of the lot. On top of his illness, he was worried about the family, especially the two girls who died, and God Himself would pity him the way he was. We all got better bit by bit but when my father was on his feet again what do you think but a policeman came with a warrant for him and the poor man scarcely able to walk even then. He had to appear in court at Falcarragh and he got six months in prison for having the potheen in his house. There was no use in his trying to deny it; he told the truth and that's what happened to him. He hadn't a word of English, the poor man, so they were able to do what they liked with him. They brought him straight over to the prison and didn't give him a smoke or anything else for the six months he was there. By the time that was finished, he was nearly dead and I can tell you he didn't do much good afterwards the short time he lived.

AT MAGHERAROARTY SCHOOL

We were left high and dry then, a big family young and weak and it wasn't easy to find us a bit of food or a stitch of clothes. Even so, my mother wanted us to get a little bit of learning if it was only that we'd be able to write a bit of a letter home when we'd be gone away. She knew well that we'd have to go as there wasn't a penny to be earned at home. Older people had been going to and from Scotland for years and they were always complaining that they were looked down on because they had neither education nor English. So I was sent to school.

The school was at Magheraroarty and it was a harsh enough place to be in. There was hardly any roof on it and, any day it would be raining, the children would be ruined. As for myself, I hadn't a single word of English no more than anyone else in my family and I couldn't answer the master when he asked me what was my name. But if I hadn't a word of English, I'd say the master hadn't a word of Irish. It wasn't for the good of the local people he had been sent up but to give some education to the children of the 'Watermen'. English was all that they had and they understood everything he had to say; but a crowd of us were sitting in our seats with neither book nor pen and we might just as well have been out on Inishdooey minding sheep. There was the master tearing away at a great rate and he would spend long periods teaching Latin to those who had English. He didn't worry himself much about us and whatever learning I got on my tongue—and I tell you that wasn't much—I'd say that it was in spite of him and in spite of myself I learned it.

HOW I LEARNED THE ALPHABET

There was an old fellow, Sean Johnny, who lived nearby and would come in to us sitting around and talking and he had spent some time in one of the hedge-schools that used to be in the neighbourhood long ago. He had a fair store of learning and he used to teach us a bit. It's from him I learned the alphabet and it was funny enough how I did that. There wasn't a house in Cloghaneely that hadn't a flagged floor then with a couple of pieces of board in the middle where they would stand the churns when they were making butter. When they were pounding potatoes, too, they would stand the pot on these boards also.

Whenever Sean would come into the house, we would be hanging out of him, urging him to tell us stories and to do some tricks for us. He'd send one of us out for a willow rod. He'd then stick the top of it in the fire and when it was blackened, he'd sit down beside the boards that were in the floor, the rest of us sitting around his feet listening. Then he'd start drawing pictures on the boards. He would outline the letters of the alphabet and name the things they resembled: A, the joining (of the roof-beams); B, spectacles; C, the moon; D, the bow and arrow; E, the gate; F, the scythe; and so on until he would have made a picture of every letter and got us to name them as he was making them. It wasn't long until we had all the letters by heart and that's something we wouldn't have been able to do with the master himself teaching us for a year. Between the two of them, anyhow, I got together a little bit of learning and there was no place I went to for the rest of my life that I wasn't able to send an account home of where I was and what I was doing.

MINDING THE COWS

I wasn't very big when I was sent off to work and what I was put to do was to mind cattle. The little parcels of land weren't divided at that time like they are now. They were all what you might call allotments—everybody had a bit here and there around the village and you might have to go through land belonging to three or four people before you came to a field of your own. This was troublesome. The only division between these allotments was a thin strip of grass-covered turf—what is called a mere in English. It wasn't so bad in winter when there was nothing growing but, from sowing time to harvest, it was necessary to stay continually with the animals. These divisions gave rise to a good deal of quarrelling and fighting between good neighbours. Hens would ruin what had been sown and I recall red war going on over that. However, I kept a sharp eye on our hens and they didn't do much damage while I was in control.

Apart from the trouble that the division into allotments gave, the tending of animals was simple enough in my time, but before that it was the custom for people to take their cattle up the mountains for grazing. It mustn't have been long since this custom had stopped for I heard of people in our own village who would take their cattle up every summer to Dunlewy in Gweedore. A couple of households would go together and build a few huts with sods out there on the hill where they would spend the summer. The women would bring their spinning wheels, their wool and their cards and they'd weave and tease the wool and run together some clothes. They would have their churns also and they would churn the milk and put the butter aside until it was time to return to the village sometime in November or beforehand.

Some of the mountainy people were accustomed to send their cattle down to the sea betimes for about six weeks. These cows from the mountain usually grazed on sedge and heather and were prone to a disease called 'crupan'; it did them good to put them on pasture by the sea. An aunt of mine was married in Dunlewy and there wasn't a year that she didn't come down with her cattle that way after August. The cattle liked no forage better than plenty of the yellow blossoms that you get in potato patches and there were plenty of those at that time. They grew both in the potato patches and in the corn and in other places where they weren't wanted; but if they did, it was my job not to let the cattle in after them.

II

On the Lagan

THE HIRING FAIR

I wouldn't like to say that I was any better as a herd than the other boys in Cloghaneely but I know this: that I had accomplished little—apart from the help I gave the potheen-makers and maybe learning the alphabet—when it was May in the year 1874. All the boys from the villages were making for Letterkenny for the hiring fair—one of four similar fairs that were held there each year. In those days, the people from the Lagan were looking for boys that would herd and give a bit of service around the house and for bigger boys that would help in the agricultural work.

I hadn't even reached my ninth year by then. I had hardly got into trousers and I don't suppose I would have been in them even then but that my mother had already resolved to send me off. All boys at that time wore petticoats until they were grown, sturdy lads. But a few nights before the fair, my aunt came over from Dunlewy with a new homespun suit for me and that was the first suit I wore and the last one I wore until I was able to buy one for myself. The day before the fair, my mother bound my little bit of baggage up in a kerchief of the kind that women wore then and, when she had done a bit of tidying around the house, herself and myself set

14

off for Letterkenny. What she intended to do was to spend the night on the way, near Doon Well where she had friends—a household of the Sweeney family, I'm thinking, and nice kind people, too. We walked out through Muckish Gap—that was the old way to Letterkenny—past Meenadrain and on with us until we got to Doon Well. My mother said that we would have to do the station* at the well before we went any further. I was tired and hungry by then and to tell the truth I had no great desire to engage in prayer. But my mother started the station and not once but three times she did it before we left the holy place behind us. And she wasn't even satisfied with that: she drank some of the water and took a bottle from under her shawl and filled it so that she could take it home with her.

We moved towards our friends' house then. Everybody was very busy at this time of the year and it was their habit to go to bed very early and rise with the dawning of the day. They were just like the birds of the air except that they were rather more mundane. As soon as we had something to eat, the old woman in the house said that we had better say the rosary then—as I looked tired, which I believed. All of us went down on our knees and it was the old woman who started off. Fifteen decades were said. I was lively enough while this lasted but when she started on the little prayers afterwards, it seemed that she was never going to stop. I was on my knees by a little oaken stool and I didn't notice a thing until I knocked my forehead on it. That wakened me up. The old woman prayed for the seven generations that preceded her, for the neighbours and those who were away in foreign parts, for protection against sickness, against devils of the earth and air, against any other harm that might be hanging over us and over the house we were in, that God might scatter and exterminate them in trees and stones far from us. I never heard the like of it for praying.

I fell into a deep sleep and neither heard nor felt anything until my mother rolled me from side to side in the bed in the morning. 'Micky, darlin',' she said, 'it's time to be getting up so that we can take to the road again.'

*Doon Well is the site of a holy well and it is customary 'to do the station' there, i.e. to pray by the well and do the special devotional exercises.

I got up. We had a bit of breakfast and set out for the big town. It was a fine morning and, in about an hour and a half, we came to the Old Town in Letterkenny. That's where the fair used to be held. There were crowds there—old and young, men, women and children. Others of my own age were there just like—though not comparing them—sheep at a fair. The big men from the Lagan were there walking about amongst us and sometimes one of them would come over to us and strike one of us between the shoulder-blades and say something to his companions about us. I remember to this day what one of them said about myself. He came over to me, caught me by the two shoulders and shook me well. 'He's a sturdy wee fellow,' he said to the man with him. At the time, I didn't know what the words meant but I remembered them and it wasn't long until I found out.

The end of the story was that two men came over to my mother and started to make a bargain with her. One of them had plenty of Irish and I think the other man had brought him with him to translate. They offered a wage of a pound for me from then until November. They went into a long story about the care that would be taken of me, about the food I would get, that I would be looked after just like one of themselves, and I don't know what else they said. My mother wasn't satisfied to let me go with them for a pound but the end of the story is that the bargain was made for thirty shillings from then until November. My new master then told me where to wait until he would be ready to collect me. Between times, my mother and myself went to an eating-house and we both had something to eat.

Up to then, I hadn't felt at all sad. But shortly now, my mother and I would be separated from each other. Up to then, everything was fresh and wonderful. The big houses and the shops and the crowds of people had taken my mind off what was before me but now a great wave of grief enveloped me. I had no further interest in anything. I was sitting on the chair in the eating-house as if my breath was choking me. The oppression was rising like water filling a bottle until at last it reached the top. I tried not to let on, however, but my mother was well aware of it. Young as I was, I noticed that. I would steal a look at her from time to time and I saw that she was tightening up her face as if a dagger was going through her heart. But she was as brave as I was except that we fell into a long silence.

I had got all necessary advices by this time: not to forget to say my prayers morning and night; to go to bed early at night; to be mannerly; always to be humble; and a whole litany of other things. You would think, really, that she didn't expect to see me again until I was a grown boy. But she was parting with her son and I suppose that there's no grief on earth is worse or more wounding than when mothers part with their sons— particularly when the son is such a little fellow.

The end came at last. In came my master and he said that it was time for us to be getting along the road. I didn't know until then what way I was going. A horse and gig were out at the door and when I went out I saw that the Irish speaker who had helped to make the bargain was sitting in the gig. That gave me some encouragement as I thought this man would be near me and if things were going hard with me I'd be able to talk to him. I got up in the gig and the tears flowed freely as I said goodbye to my mother. I was on my way to the Lagan.

The people of Cloghaneely at that time called anywhere eastwards, from Muckish Mountain to Co. Antrim, the 'Lagan'. That part of the country hadn't got a very good reputation in our neighbourhood. When anyone referred to the 'Lagan', it meant slavery, struggle, extortion and work from morning till night. All the stories I had heard about it were wheeling around in my mind as the horse was trotting up the street of Letter-kenny. My heart gave a jump when I saw the driver turning the horse towards the left hand. He drove on and it wasn't long until we were on the old back road to Errigal between Termon and Gweedore.

The Irish speaker—I found out that he was an O'Donnell— was a great companion. There wasn't a story about this historic district that he didn't relate to me: Doon Well, where everyone that passed by, did the station; Doon Rock above it, where the Princes of the O'Donnells were crowned; Gartan, where Columbkille was born and where his traces were still to be found in church and stone—I heard the whole history on this journey.

GLENVEAGH

At last we reached our journey's end—in Glenveagh—and came to the door of the house where I was to spend six months as a young herd. They gave me a right good welcome; and what comforted me most, even before I sat down, was to find that there was an old woman in the house who spoke the most limpid Irish. Not that I talked very much that evening. I was over-tired and, when I had something to eat, I washed my feet and went to bed. I slept well on this, my first night 'on the continent', and it was no bother to me to get up in the morning and start work. I was up good and early and looked around the neighbourhood before anybody else wakened up. When I got back, they were all up and there was a fine pot of hot stirabout ready. There was some fine fresh milk too and, between that and the stirabout, I couldn't quarrel with it as a breakfast. In those days, tea was scarce enough in our part of the country and, apart from a drop on Sundays or on some festive occasion, we didn't have it very often.

When breakfast was over, the man of the house—Paddy O'Donnell by name—took me out and, from the cowshed beside the house, he brought out a fine herd of cattle, and told me to look after them. 'It's not hard,' he said, 'but the hill is full of holes and there's always the danger that one of the cows would stick her foot in one of them and break her leg.'

I drove the cattle on until I brought them to the place where the man of the house told me to bring them. They had plenty of grazing there and it wasn't at all difficult to look after them. I climbed a little hillock nearby and looked around. Right in front of me there was one of the most beautiful sights that anyone ever saw. It wasn't the kind of landscape that I was used to at home. I missed the sea and the islands and there wasn't the same green countryside around me. I was in a mountainy desert. All I saw around me were mountains and valleys, lakes and streams, heather, rushes and sedge; but the wild beauty of the place made my heart rise. I noticed a couple of things that made me wonder; one, that there were very few houses around and, the other, that there was a police barracks there. I thought that it was a backward kind of a place to have a barracks in but I wasn't long in the place until the old woman told me the whole story about it.

BLACKFACED SHEEP AND RED-COATED SOLDIERS

Sometime before I was born, a 'gentleman' came to Glenveagh. In those days, anybody that came by the way with any kind of decent clothes on him and a store of English was called a 'gentleman'. John George Adair was the name of this man. He liked our remote part of the country so much that he lost many a night's sleep wondering how he could get possession of it. Sometime during 1858, he managed to buy a large portion of the land and of the nearby mountain. That was the black day for Glenveagh and a day that's not forgotten to this moment in the history of the district. There wasn't a day's ease or peace in the glen from that time onwards.

About the time that Adair was squeezing the people of Glenveagh, those in Gweedore and Cloghaneely and west to Glencolumbkille were having trouble about the 'black-faced sheep'. The landlords of these parishes were told that if they got rid of their tenants and covered the hills with black-faced sheep of Scottish stock, they'd make their fortune in no time. As they used to say in the old stories long ago, the giants were greedy for gold—and they brought in the sheep. You might say that the cat was among the pigeons then. The people were dissatisfied and no wonder. The main support of the people in this area were the few sheep that they would raise on the mountains and that they would sell from time to time as they were hungry or had to meet rent and taxes or get a bit of food for themselves and their children.

The good Adair had his share of the black-faced sheep. He brought in herdsmen from Scotland, building houses and everything else for them. But he started losing sheep practically immediately and the tenants were being blamed by the herdsmen for the stealing and killing. This, of course, didn't do Adair any good, particularly as the truth of the matter was that the sheep were dying from neglect, bad weather and general wretchedness. To cap it all, one of Adair's servants named Murray was accidentally killed and this drove him out of his mind altogether—there was no holding him after that.

It was about this time that the barracks that I saw and admired was built. When it was built, the police were stationed there to guard Adair and to save him from the 'wild men of the hills' as he called them. He swore then that there wasn't any mother's son in the area that he wouldn't drive from hearth and home. He demanded two hundred police and the same number of red-coats (soldiers) for this dirty work. Well, he got them: one day in the month of February, 1861, there they were, armed to the teeth. Up to then, none of the tenants believed that he'd be pitiless enough to throw them out, leaving them without a house, a shed, a hovel or shelter of any kind for themselves or their children. But he didn't care what happened to them and he threw them out on the road-side in their hundreds without food, drink or clothing. Surely God himself was watching the way they were left—and what matter if they had deserved it—standing out there, the poor creatures, while the soldiers of the queen levelled their houses to the ground. Neither the neighbours, nor anyone else with a shred of pity or Christianity in their hearts, failed at this time. They all came and formed a little committee and between themselves and a few friends that they had in Australia, they got together and collected enough money to send these poor people out there. None of them ever returned.

I don't think I've ever heard any story worse than that and I've never forgotten the grief of the old woman who told it to me. She remembered all the details and there were relations of hers involved that she never saw again. They would write to her frequently and, heavy and all as their hearts may have been, they were doing well and, in their letters, their only complaint was that the heat was killing them!

THE FRIENDLY CONSTABLE

There wasn't a day that went by that I wasn't getting to know the place and the people better. Now and again, the cows I was minding would move over near the barracks at Meenadrain and I'd be there on the roadside looking after them. There were a lot of police there with nothing to do apart from keeping an eye on the castle that Adair built for himself on the shores of Lough Veagh. Among them was a fine young man named Sean McDonnell from Armagh. Not a day would go by that he wouldn't come over to me and we'd have a fine long chat. If he didn't bring a cup of tea over to me from the barracks, he'd leave it for me there and mind the cows until I returned. The first time I went to the barracks I was terrified because I thought they'd keep me there, especially when one of the police showed me the 'prison' they had. That feeling didn't last long, however, and in no time I was feeling very confident. I found out that the police hated the people they were working for just as much as most in the area did. Needless to say, most of them didn't like being in that remote part of the country and they swore fluently enough about the people in the castle who were responsible for their being there.

THE STONE OF HOMESICKNESS

Everybody was very good to me in Glenveagh but seeing that I was, after all, only a child, it's no wonder that I'd get very sad from time to time. The old woman that was in the house was always telling stories and yarning and I gave her good ear. Mostly they were stories with a religious turn. She had fine stories about Columbkille and about Doon Well and other holy places in or about Gartan. One night I was listening to her telling about the place in Gartan where the saint was born. It can still be seen there, the stone on which he came into the world. 'The Stone of Homesickness' or 'Columbkille's Stone' it is called; and it is said that anybody who is going from home, or who is away from home and is sad, and who goes to the stone and lies down on it, will not feel lonely ever again.

Sorrows enough I had myself at that time. They would only overcome me now and again and, even then, mainly when I'd be going to bed at night. I had, too—and still have—a sort of fear of ghosts and didn't like to be by myself too much at night-time. Sunday—a day when I hadn't too much heavy work—was drawing near and one night I resolved that if God left me my health I'd go then to Gartan and try to get cured.

Sunday came and I don't think there was ever a more beautiful day. There was only some light work to be done and when it was finished and my bit of dinner eaten, I told the people in the house that I was going off to Gartan. I was afraid to go anywhere without letting them know where I'd be. The man of the house gave me directions about the shortest way to get there and, indeed, it wasn't all that far if I went across the hill. I hadn't either socks or boots and I went over that hill as fast as a greyhound. Not a sinner did I meet on the way. In front of me and to the right lay the countryside that had been laid waste some years beforehand. There wasn't a sign of human life but you could feel the landscape palpitating with the ghosts of the poor wretches that had been driven off it. I made down the other side of the hill and I came by the bushes that the man of the house had told me about. He had told me also about the big Celtic Cross that Mrs. Adair had raised beside the Stone and said I'd have no trouble in finding the Stone itself. I reached it alright—a big rough Stone with holes in it that you could put your fingers in. I stretched on that Stone that saw Columbkille's birth, if the story is true, and the happiness that Columbkille has in heaven was nothing to the happiness that came over me that day.

The bramble-bushes around the place provided a fine shelter. The sun was shining warmly and when I stretched out on the stone, it wasn't long until I forgot the world all around and didn't I fall into a deep sleep! Whether I slept there on the flat of my back for a long or a short time I do not know but what wakened me was the noise made by a man in the field next to me as he drove his cows home. I started up then and no grass grew under my feet until I was safely back in again. It was twilight by the time I finished my supper and when I drew water and turf in for the night I went off to bed. Not a worry was on me that night as I slept soundly.

I RETURN HOME

I worked away in Meenadrain and, in the end, it was just like being among my own people back in Cloghaneely. The work wasn't heavy—light tasks, going to the shop and so forth—and, as November drew near, what began to worry me was that I'd have to be moving home. November came but instead of my going back to Letterkenny where I was hired, my mother came to collect me. I was disappointed at this for, to be honest, I had been looking forward to another visit to that town. While I was 'on hire', the people in the house and the neighbours would give me a few pence from time to time and since I'd had no chance of spending them, I'd a fine, heavy purse, and I thought that in Letterkenny I'd be able to buy something. I was the most dissatisfied boy in the world when my mother said that we'd take the short cut through Muckish Gap. My wages were paid to my mother. We said goodbye to Meena-drain and headed back towards Pollanaranny. I'd had my first taste of working in service—and of the world.

I spent a while just running around the village. You'd think I'd returned from America, there was such a welcome given to me. When I'd go into the neighbours' houses, I'd have to go straight up to the ingle-nook where the old women were. After shaking hands with me, they'd turn me around on the floor examining me up and down: I'd grown a lot; I'd got fat; I'd changed a lot; I didn't resemble my father nearly as much as I did six months before; then they'd remark that I was in the money now—at which we'd all laugh.

For about a week after my return, I went around like that but then one day my mother said that I'd have to go back to school for another while. I'd have been just about as pleased if she told me that I had to go to the gallows. It was no use, however, to say that I wouldn't go. In those days, children had to do what they were told. I went back to school alright but, if I did, I didn't learn much. There was a lot of strong growing lads there without a care in the world who spent their time throwing sods at one another or wrestling and they were so big and hefty that the master was afraid to interfere with them. There was a crowd at the school that winter that were as strong and as tough as they'd ever be.

I passed the winter by way of being at school, so to speak, but with the beginning of spring, there wasn't a day dawned that the number of pupils didn't grow smaller. The days for digging were near and once St. Patrick's Day was over there was always something to be done at home. I suppose our people thought that it was only a waste of time to have us at school. I stayed home at the beginning of March. My brother Jimmy, who was older than I, had already spent a couple of seasons in Scotland. He, too, would spend the winter at home and he liked to leave some turf cut and some seed sown before he left again. When that was done, he'd leave; and shortly afterwards, I'd have to set out, just the same as before, for the Lagan.

BACK ON THE LAGAN

May-day came and I was off. I was wiser than I had been a year previously and as well as that, I understood English better. However, my mother brought me to Letterkenny again this time. We didn't go by Doon Well or call on the Sweeney family as we had done before but made straight for an old woman from Cloghaneely named Mary McCaffrey who lived in Letterkenny. She always had room at her house for anyone from our parish who was at the hiring fair. There wasn't much space in the house but at least it was shelter for the night. Everybody knew Mary and as dusk began to fall the house filled with people. There was someone there from every district in the county and particularly from the Irish-speaking areas. Everyone from those parts knew that she would speak Irish and those who hadn't much English would come straight to her. Very shortly, her house was as full as if there was a wake there. She refused nobody that came to her door and they were all there old and young. She couldn't provide beds for them all but some of the people didn't care about the beds as long as they had the shelter. The conversation and the story-telling started then and it wasn't long until everybody knew each other. It's wonderful how quickly people who are moving away from home like that get to know one another. By ten o'clock that night everybody was chatting away as if they had known the people next to them all their lives.

Among the crowd, there was a small mettlesome old man, Micky McGlynn, who had spent most of his life 'in service'. He was very knowledgeable about life and there was nothing going on around the Lagan area that he didn't know about. He came from the area around the Glenties and, with the store of knowledge he had about the Lagan and the world in general, he was a fine story-teller. He told a story that night that he called 'The Great Wheel of Life'—a strange story that I never heard before nor since. I never forgot it and I often thought afterwards that there was a great deal in it that resembled my own story.

It was a story about a boy who was an only child. The father was hot-tempered and tyrannical and used to give the mother a terrible life. The boy got sick and tired of this and left the house altogether. He obtained shelter from a wealthy farmer that had a son of about his own age. The farmer was very good to him and as he was a very clever boy the two of them used have long discussions about life. One subject the boy used draw down very frequently was the strange mutability of life. 'It's very queer,' he'd say, 'this life. It's like a great big wheel going round. The person who's at the top of the wheel this year is likely enough to be at the bottom next year and the person who's at the bottom this year may well be at the top next year.'

'It's true enough for you,' said the farmer.

The farmer sent the boy to college and in seven years he became a priest. He came home then to find that his father was dead and that he was just in time to see his mother before she passed away. While he was saying the prayers over his mother, a loud noise was heard above the cottage and when he looked up what did he see but his own father that had been buried for seven years. His father told him that he wouldn't be let near to Heaven because of his bad conduct on earth, that he was obliged to wander about without ease or peace and that it was likely that he'd have to stay like that for eternity. A lot of the story then related how the young priest spent twenty-one years in a mud-hut on the top of the highest hill in the county doing penance for his father and how he managed to save him in the end.

The priest was very good to the poor and he gave alms one day to a poor miserable wretch who came to his hovel. The old man told the priest his story—about the fine place he had once upon a time, about his own son and about the boy stranger that he had sent to college and whom he hadn't seen after that. He told the priest how the boy stranger used compare life to a revolving wheel and how some would be up or down as it went around.

'When I had that boy,' he said, 'I was comfortable and everything was going well with me. My wife died, however, and after that my stock started to diminish like the mist on the hill and the end of it all was that I was left poor and cold and I had to take to the roads begging my bit from door to door. The wheel turned in my case just as the boy stranger used to say.'

'Well, I'm the boy you reared,' said the priest, 'and you won't go from me now for as long as you live. The wheel has turned again.'

And the old man spent the rest of his life happily with the priest.

It was a wonderful story, I thought, but you'd have to hear Micky McGlynn telling it in full to appreciate it properly.

We didn't sleep much that night and it was hardly day when everybody started gathering in the market-place of the fair. There were farmers there from every quarter of Ulster. They probably thought that they'd get people like us from the western parts cheaply enough and they knew, of course, the reputation we had: that we were as good workers as could be got in the whole country. I was myself as hard-working as any you'd find. This was my second year and it's amazing the change that a year makes in a boy. The year before I was practically hanging out of the tassels of my mother's shawl but this time I was running around on my own and having little conversations in English with the Lagan people. Indeed, their accent and idiom was hard to follow: it was not the same as what the master who taught me at school had. When they'd be talking about boys such as myself, 'bairns', they'd call them. One man was telling about a horse that took fright as she was being led to the fair that morning and what he said was that the animal was 'copin' curly'. Another man averred that he was 'sagged with the rheumatics' and that we were lucky to have 'suchan a brave day'. When I heard all this, and more,

I was of the opinion that it would be just as easy for them to understand my Irish as it was for me to make head or tail of their English.

To make a long story short, I was hired to a man from Drumoghill called Sam Duv*, a fine well-built man with a red forehead and a large hooked nose. It wasn't hard to know from his face and bearing that he was a Lutheran. But if he was big, he was kindly too, and there was no more harm in him than there would be in a child. He had a horse and car with him and when the day's business was over, he harnessed the horse and started for home. There were three or four others with him—men younger than himself who hadn't anything to do at the fair except to look around them there. We weren't long on the road for Drumoghill is only about five miles on the Lifford side of Letterkenny. There's fine country all around there and it's as good growing country as you'll get in Ireland. In my day, it was all 'Scotsmen'† who were there, but I heard that it has much changed and that some of our own people were now getting the places that their forefathers had been driven from.

SAM DUV AND YELLOW JANE

Without too much delay, we reached Sam's house. It was a bit off the main road and as we came by the door a big blonde woman came out and grabbed hold of the horse's head. I eyed her closely. The clothes she had on filled me with amazement. She wore a man's old cap that the peak had been torn from at some stage and a man's jacket, and from there to her boots she was covered in an old raggy apron made from potato sacking. She wore man's boots as well and if they were an inch long they were a foot and a half. I'd swear they hadn't been cleaned from the day they left the shop. I often heard tell while I was at home of superstitious old women that would drag a straw rope after them in the dew on a May morning hoping to draw to themselves their neighbour's milk and butter. Without lie or exaggeration, I thought in my heart that it was one of these women that now held the horse's head.

We got down from the cart, Sam took the horse's head and

*Black-haired. †Presbyterians.

introduced me to the hag. Jane was her name and herself and
Sam were brother and sister. Jane told me to follow her into
the house. I went after her and found the same untidy way
about the kitchen as there was about herself. There was an old
log in the fireplace that stuck out into the middle of the floor;
over it a pot hung in which there were potatoes being boiled
for the pigs while another pot and a tub hung in the ingle-nook
also. You'd sink up to your ankles in dirt of every kind on the
floor. Apart from the pots and the tub, I don't believe that there
was any vessel in the kitchen that wasn't on a table over at the
side of the house and, to add to the confusion, there were a
dozen or so hens picking and scratching in the refuse that was
on the floor. This, I thought to myself, is a hard house.

Well, that was all right. Sam put the horse in the stable and
came in. He spoke to the hag and though I didn't fully understand what he said I knew it was something about getting us
some food. She cleared the top of the table then and pulled
over the pot that was beside the fire. She took a bowl that was
on the table, filled it with potatoes and left it back on the table.
She then went over to the churn and filled from it two bowls of
buttermilk which she left with us. The potatoes were cold and
although I was starving with the hunger it wasn't with any
pleasure I ate them. While we ate, the old hag sat at the top of
the table with a dishcloth in her hand with which she endea-
voured to keep the hens off the table. She was trying to make
me talk at the same time but I hardly understood a word she
said no more than if she was speaking Greek to me. I 'yessed'
and 'no'd' and that's about all there was to it.

When the food was eaten, the man of the house asked me
to go out with him to see the holding and the stock. There was
a little garden behind the house in which there was a sow with
a litter of bonnaves* of which there must have been at least a
dozen. Down from the house there was a large meadow with
upwards of a score of bullocks in it while below that again
there was another field with four milch cows in it. I said a few
words of praise both about the place and the stock but really I
kept my own counsel about what I saw. I knew that there
would be a lot of hard work for me from then on.

*Young pigs.

Nothing much was said to me that night about the actual work and after I was given a bowl of stirabout I was shown my bed. There was no talk about the rosary like the O'Donnells in Meenadrain, and I remember that, foolishly enough, I went looking for holy water before I turned in. But, as the saying has it, I could have been looking for it in hell. The room in which I was put wasn't too well provided for either. It held an old wooden bed and, on my word, there are people alive now that wouldn't even put a dog to lie on the bed-clothes that were there. It wasn't quite a sack that was on the bed but something like it and that was the blanket I wrapped myself up in that first night I returned to the Lagan. All the same, I slept as soundly as if I was lying on a bed of birds' feathers until morning.

The old hag didn't sleep much, as far as I could see. She started screeching early enough and daylight was hardly there before she was rampaging around the house. To give her her due, she didn't bother me but when I heard the row she was kicking up I thought I better get up. I jumped out, threw on my clothes and came down to the kitchen. There was Jane before me heating a pot of stirabout for breakfast. She gave me a bowl and a mug of milk that was as sour as a crab-apple. It wouldn't have done me any good to have said anything. I thought to myself that it would be better to wait until I knew her better. It wouldn't do to start a row on my very first day there. Sam, who had been out looking after the cows came in just then and sat down and he didn't seem to find anything wrong with the fare. But, of course, he had a 'Scotsman's' swallow and he'd have eaten the stones of the fields so long as they were soft enough.

MILKING THE COWS

The time came then to start working. Jane asked me if I could milk a cow. I told her that I had never been under a cow in my life. 'Well, lazyboots,' she said, 'you can't start to learn early enough. I'll be in charge of you and if you're going to be here, you'll have to be able to get under them. There was never a boy in this house that hadn't to milk.' All the time Jane was telling me what I'd have to do, she was standing in the middle of the floor and there was never an actor on any stage that had as many gestures as she had. She shook her head so much that you'd think if it wasn't so well attached she'd lose it. As well as telling me about the cows and the work that went with them—which included helping her with the churning, a job I wasn't supposed to have to do—there were messages to be run, eggs to be brought to the shop, herding, firing to be collected (faggots mostly they burned), pig-food to be prepared and I don't know what else. All together, I tell you it looked likely that I wouldn't spend too much time talking to the gulls!

There was no point in making a song and dance out of it—I started in to work, by helping Jane to milk the cows. I belted away in fine style to begin with but my little hands were weak and it wasn't long until my wrists were hurting. I had to keep on just the same and it wasn't long until I got the knack tired though I was. When I finished my service with Sam, I was— though I shouldn't say it myself—probably one of the best milkers in the whole county.

GOING TO THE SHOP

There was no work no matter how hard it was that I wasn't ready for—except taking the eggs to the shop. I might as well have been going to the gallows as going there. I thought everybody's eye was on me, going along the road there with a big basket of eggs on my arm; for the most part, it was the very old men that went with the eggs and I hated this so much that I would have run straight home if the shopkeeper hadn't been so good to me. When he got to know me, there wasn't a day that I'd visit him that he wouldn't fill my pockets with sweets and, in the end, Jane couldn't ask me often enough to go. Whenever I'd collect groceries for her, I'd never get any change. The change would be left with the shopkeeper and then about once a month she'd go along herself to collect it. When she'd get home, she'd put every halfpenny in a little bag with a draw-string on it. Not a farthing would come out of that bag again. Halfpennies were worth something in those days and Jane would make prisoners of every one that came her way. Both herself and Sam were so stingy and miserly that God alone knew when they last had a change of clothing—they couldn't bring themselves to spare the cost. And it's not that they hadn't got it: they had stacks of money and I never heard what they did with it; neither of them married and they didn't leave any close relatives behind them.

THE 'SCOTTISH' STORY-TELLER

I spent the summer slogging away there in Drumoghill. There was no ease or satisfaction in the place at all, working away from morning to night on poor food and sleeping on a most uncomfortable bed. However, I was young, I fell in with the strange little habits of Sam and Jane and the hardship didn't worry me too much. They were kind enough in their own way —it was as if they had never known anything better. In some ways they were better than their neighbours—they had no ill-will towards Catholics, for instance. Come Sunday morning, if I wasn't up myself, they'd call me and tell me it was time to dress myself to go to the 'kirk' as they called the church. As a result of that, when I grew older and went out in the world, my respect for the old pair grew. They didn't worry themselves too much about churches of any kind. The minister would come to the house now and again and I believe he'd read them something called 'the lesson', but I'd be sent out while he'd be there.

As Our Lady's Day passed, the nights started to lengthen and the neighbours would come in. Material cares worried them more than anything else but now and again there'd be great nights of story-telling and a wealth of tales would be told. There was one old man in particular named Billy Craig who came visiting regularly and I can't tell you the number of stories he had. He'd have been nearing eighty at this time and he was one of those who spent the early part of his life going around the province of Ulster ploughing in the spring-time. He had a great reputation as a ploughman. I think it was because of all his wandering that he had the gift of story-telling. I often heard people say since then that the 'Scots' had no lore or superstitions but I can tell you they're wrong. Billy Craig had plenty of lore and stories just like some of our own people and he was as superstitious as any of the old people that you'd ever meet. Sam and Jane were just the same.

When Billy would come to the house at twilight, he'd get his back in the corner and, if the king himself was to come in, he wouldn't move from there until bed-time. He was a heavy smoker and when he'd get the pipe going he wouldn't be silent as long as there was anyone to listen to him. There was no kind of story-telling that he didn't know something about but he specialized in stories about ghosts and the 'little people'.* It's likely enough that he believed in ghosts because if he was to stay till morning he wouldn't leave the house without a companion although he lived only a short distance away.

I heard him say that the 'little people' left the district we were in about twenty years beforehand. He said he was very friendly with an old woman, Curly Mary, to whom the 'little people' would come now and again and they told her the night they'd be leaving the place. They said that the fairy hosts of Connaught had declared war on them and that they had to go and fight them. If they lost, they said to the old woman, the well from which she drew water would be red with blood in the morning. Sometime after that there was a night of terrible thunder and lightning and the following morning when Curly Mary went out for a pail of water, there was the well red with blood. She knew then that the fairy host from Connaught had won and from that day forward the 'little people' never returned either to Drumoghill or to the whole province of Ulster.

There was no end to the stories that Billy had about this aery throng—stories about everything pertaining to them: people they helped and people they hurt; people they took away and who never returned; people who felled trees or bushes in some sacred place and who never did any good afterwards; people who built houses in forbidden places; people who threw water on the doorstep and who were advised not to be trying to drown the fairies; people who learned music from them and people who didn't like their music and whom they turned into hunchbacks. Many is the night I spent listening to these stories about fairies and ghosts and when I'd be going to bed, I'd be squeezing myself up like a handkerchief thinking,

*The fairies.

as I went to my room, that I'd find the place full of them .It would be the same when I'd be sent out herding. There wasn't a bush or a hillock around but I'd expect to see one of these little youths standing behind it. Maybe it was all these stories of Billy's that made me so nervous in the end.

I said that both Sam and Jane were superstitious and that's nothing but the truth. I saw Sam tying a red tassel around the neck of a calf that he was letting out for the first time. I saw Jane take a piece of fresh butter out of the churn and stick it to the wall over the cattle. She did this to save the milk from evil charms; and, of course, there was a horse-shoe on the door of the cow-house with the heel part upwards. I thought nobody paid any attention to these customs except at home but I was finding out that the people in the Lagan were, if anything, more superstitious than our own.

Be that as it may, I stayed there until November. When the day came on which I had decided to go home, Sam besought me to stay with him but I think that even if he had given me all he had, I wouldn't have stayed another week. I was delighted to be on my way home. When he saw that it was no use, he told Jane to give me my wages. It was she who handled the money. She handed over my thirty shillings and I don't think that any boy ever put such well-earned money into his pocket. I didn't mind that as I'd have it all to give over to my mother when I got home. I had no pocket money this time unlike the season I spent in Glenveagh. I used to get little bits of change and the odd few pennies from the shopping there, but I never got as much as one halfpenny from Jane.

Sam was going into Letterkenny with the horse and he gave me a lift that far. There were plenty of people there that I knew well but we made no delay till we reached the road back of Errigal and were well on our way home.

III

In Scotland

SURREPTITIOUS DEPARTURE

By the time I was fifteen I had spent five or six seasons on the
Lagan. Many a different kind of master and mistress I had from
season to season. I met a lot of interesting people and a lot of
strange things happened to me. There was good and bad
everywhere I went, but none of the places was any too easy.
But repetition makes a story dull and I'll say no more about
that.

About this time, myself and a young relative of mine, Conal
Eileen* by name, were great friends. We saw that we had
nothing to gain by going again and again to the Lagan and
we made it up between us that we'd both go to Scotland like
most of the younger people of Cloghaneely did at that time.
St. Patrick's Day, 1880, I think it was. Anybody that had a
penny in his pocket was merry enough that night and there
was a fair amount of noise going on. That, we thought, was the
best night to be off. We were a bit afraid of saying that we were
off to Scotland in case we mightn't be let go. If our fathers were
going with us nobody would bother us but, alas! that wasn't
the case. We knew that we wouldn't be missed that blessed
night for a long time and, as well as that, that our people

*In Irish, the second name is the name of either the father or the mother.

34

would know, when we'd be missing in the morning, that we were gone to Scotland. We'd be a good way from home then and there'd be no point in pursuing us. We spent a long time that morning getting together what we intended to bring with us. Having talked it over for a long time, we decided that the best way for us to leave was with our hands hanging, only taking a couple of loaves of bread with us to keep us going. In those days oatmeal bread was made in every house and I had some hidden away outside early in the afternoon. As the day drew to a close, I got very restless. I was in and out of the house and no sooner did I sit down on the stool than I'd have to get up and go out. There's nothing I resembled more than a hen that had a nest somewhere and was trying to steal out to lay unbeknownst.

Well, the night began to fall at last—a fine dry night with a south-east wind blowing up from Errigal. It looked as if it would be a good dry night and, therefore, a good night for walking. I don't know whether my mother felt that something was in the wind or not, but she seemed to me to be watching me as she might watch a robber. I was afraid, naturally, that she might notice the bit of bread missing but, if she did, she didn't say anything. I was waiting for the chance to skip away as fast as I could. I knew that it was the custom for my mother, when she had milked the cows, to take a drop of milk to one of the neighbours houses. Everything happened just as if I had ordered it and, when I saw the coast clear, I skipped off. I made for the ditch where I had hidden the bread and, as fast as I could, I made off and you may be sure no grass grew under my feet until I had left the house well behind me.

I got to the cross-roads where Conal Eileen was to meet me but when I got there there wasn't a sinner in view. I strolled around for a good while and at last he hove in sight. By the time he reached me he was pretty breathless. He had been like myself, waiting for the chance to slip away from his family and he only made it in the latter end. We said goodbye to the old place and turned our faces towards Derry.

It was nearly the middle of the night by now but there was a lot of people on the road. Some of them were roaming home after 'wetting the shamrock' and some others were going to houses where they'd spend the night dancing and making music of one kind or another. We didn't mind the first crowd as we knew they wouldn't pay any attention to us while we thought the best way we could go was to take the short cut over the hills. And that's what we did. We made out by Cashel Hill and Altatorav and Tullaghobegley until we reached the road to Muckish Gap. We were safe enough by then—nobody could catch us any more. Even if they didn't, our journey was nothing to look forward to—a walk of fifty miles and nothing in our pockets but the bare boat-fare. But we were young and lively at the time and we thought nothing of that walk no more than we'd think of a walk to Falcarragh.

Conal Eileen had spent a couple of seasons in service near Derry and he more or less knew the way. He would encourage me by saying that if we got that far someone would give us enough to eat that would get us over to Scotland. As long as we met people on the road, we knew neither fear nor loneliness but after midnight the lights went out one after another and in the end we would only see an odd one. I might as well tell the truth: from then on I was pretty well afraid all the time. If I only heard a bird flapping in the bush by the roadside, I'd jump a foot in the air. Conal was trying to keep up a bit of conversation with me but at times when he'd throw a question to me it would be a couple of minutes before I'd answer him. During that time I'd be looking here and there watching for something—what I didn't know—to jump out from the ditch at the side of the road and terrify me.

We went on, however, and as the dawn came, Conal said that we ought to make for the place where he had worked the year previous. 'God lead us to it,' I cried, 'for my feet are persecuting me and if we don't get somewhere soon, I'll have to lie down by the side of the road.'

'It's not worth your while sitting down now,' said Conal. 'As you've come so far, you might as well walk another half-mile.'

On we went. The day was getting brighter with every step we took. At last Conal stood still and looked around him.

'We're a few hundred yards from Davy Duv's house,' he said, 'or I'm a Dutchman.'

'Davy Duv,' I cried. 'I don't care if he's as black as the devil so long as he's there.'

We went ahead for about the distance Conal had mentioned and, right enough, there was the house a bit up off the road. We came up to it but the inhabitants weren't up by then. Conal said he'd knock on the door but I thought it might be better not to disturb them as they'd be getting up soon and we'd be nicely rested by the time they'd be on their feet. There was a cart-shed at the gable end of the house that had a few bottles* of hay in it and when I saw them I thought that if I could stretch out on them for a half an hour it would do me all the good in the world. Over I went and just as I was stretching myself out, there was an unmerciful noise right beside me and a huge dog sprang to bite me. Luckily enough he was tied up and the rope was short enough to prevent him reaching me. He made a terrible racket, however, and it wasn't long until the man of the house came out. He had neither boots nor socks on him and it wasn't a blessing that passed his lips as he came towards us. He had a head of hair on him like a hedge-hog and you'd swear that there wasn't a strand on his head or in his beard that wasn't standing up. The murder the dog was kicking up was nothing to the roars he was letting out of him before he got near us. By God, I thought, you ruffian. Davy Duv is more than a nickname for you!

Conal knew that this was only his outward appearance and he went over towards him. He spoke to him and immediately Davy Duv recognized him. He gave him a great welcome.

'What mischief,' he asked, 'is bringing you out at this time of the morning?'

'We're on our way to Scotland,' said Conal, 'and because I know my way around these parts, we came along here for a bit of rest.'

'Well, come on into the house,' said Davy, 'and get something to eat.'

That was a sweet song for us to hear and we didn't wait for the second invitation. While Davy was putting on his boots, I busied myself making a fine fire of what faggots there were. He then got a couple of big measures from the table at the other

*Presumably from Old French—*botel*.

37

end of the kitchen and put them on the fire. He heated them and gave us plenty of bread and butter with the hot milk. We weren't slow to assuage our hunger and when we were finished our meal we didn't care where the sun rose or set.

MY FIRST SEA JOURNEY

We spent a good while with Davy. We knew that the day would be well gone by the time the boat left Derry and it was just as well for us to spend the time with Davy as to spend it wandering around the town. In due course we strolled over to the quay of Derry. There were crowds of people getting on to the same boat—people from every corner of Donegal all bent on the same mission as ourselves. There they were, men and women, young and old, all off to Scotland looking for work to gather a bit of money to keep themselves and the families they were leaving behind them alive. You could see that the older ones, who already had tasted the foreign parts, had no great wish to be on the move again. They knew that they would have neither ease nor peace until they returned. But we were young, we didn't know any better and we were like young people going to a feast.

We got our tickets. They weren't dear then—I paid two shillings and I had a half-crown left over. A lot of time went by while they were loading up the boat with bullocks and goods; we were then put on board among the cattle and the boat made off down Lough Foyle. The grief of Columbkille leaving Ireland from the self-same harbour was hardly worth talking about when you saw the state some of those poor people on the boat were in.

Everything was right enough while we were in the channel but as soon as we got out to sea the pitching and the tossing started. The wind was blowing from the north-west against the shoulder of the ship and a heavy sea accompanied it. Even though I had been reared beside the sea, I had never put my foot in a boat before this. I was sitting in the front of the ship and when the pitching started I thought my head was getting light and that my stomach was turning over. It wasn't long until I had plenty of companions and though I was sick enough

I wasn't vomiting. God was watching the night that I spent between sickness and depression particularly from looking at those who were worse than I was. Indeed, there was one period when I longed for the ship to sink straight away to the bottom of the sea. I lay there wretched and weak and I didn't care if I never saw dry land again!

We got in to Glasgow quay sometime about six o'clock in the morning. The first question then was which direction should we go in—where would we be likely to get something to do. Conal was as ignorant as I was myself about this part of the business, but while we had been standing on the quay at Derry the day beforehand we got into conversation with a man from the Rosses—a fine man named Paddy O'Boyle. He was middle-aged and we knew by his clothes that he was going back to Scotland. We questioned him and he told us that he was working in the big iron works at Coatbridge. He had been there for years and was well satisfied with it. Coatbridge is in Lanarkshire about nine or ten miles east from Glasgow. The Baird Company built the Gartsherrie Iron Works there and for many a long year they were the most famous ironworks in the three kingdoms. There was nothing you could think of from nails to huge anchors that didn't come out of their enormous furnaces but if that was the case there was plenty of sweat being lost in their factories. The work was heavy and the hours long but it was better than spending half your life tramping the Lothians and down to England looking for work.

'Would we have any chance of getting a start there,' I asked O'Boyle, 'if we made our way up there?'

'Well,' he said, 'I can't give you a straight answer on that but I'm friendly with the foreman and if you come up there, I'll put in a word for you.'

EAST TO COATBRIDGE

As the people disembarked from the boat when we reached Glasgow, O'Boyle went off with himself and we didn't see any more of him at that time. We strolled up town and spent some time looking around. We saw biscuits on sale in a shop for a halfpenny each and one of them would do any man for a meal. We bought a couple each and stuck them in our pockets. After that, we put our heads together and decided that the best thing for us to do was to go east to Coatbridge. It was too early to start work on a farm and we thought we might pick up something that would do us until about the middle of the summer.

We asked and got directions and started on our way. Neither of us had the remotest idea about the country and, whether long or short the journey, we hadn't an inkling. One thing was giving me some worry. I used to hear the older people who had been to and from Scotland years before talking about a village they passed through on their way to the harvesting—a place called Armadale. In those days, people from our place used to wear breeches and great-coats made from home-spun bawneen* and no matter where they went they were recognized as being from our area. Whatever hatred the people of Armadale conceived for them, it appears that they would attack our people with bottles and stones anytime they saw them. Our men at that time had to bring their sickles over with them and they used to bind the blade with rope so that no damage would be done; but coming towards Armadale, they'd take the rope off the sickle so as to be ready to fight if the toughs of the village started attacking them. I was afraid that we might have to go by that village but, luckily enough, we didn't—it lay further on eastwards.

We didn't know that at the time, however, so we walked warily. We had a couple of pairs of old boots on us and as we weren't used to wearing them it wasn't long until our feet were hurting. Well, we sat down on the side of the road and took them off. We threw them over our shoulders and forged ahead bare-foot. Then, like the women who carried their boots going to Sunday Mass and who put them on at Colleybridge, outside Gortahork, we put ours on again outside Coatbridge. We ate the biscuits we had bought in the shop and when our repast was over we went into the town and headed for the iron-works. There was a right lot of men to be seen there and they all looked very busy. We asked for O'Boyle and a boy brought us to him. He was almost in his skin, I can tell you, loading ore as

*Homespun tweed.

fast as he could into one of the furnaces. When I saw him there bathed in sweat, I thought to myself that even if I got a job, I'd never be able to stick it for very long.

O'Boyle recognized us immediately and he called to another man to take his place while he was talking to us. He knew well, of course, what brought us there. He brought the pair of us into a little office and told the man there that we were two young fellows looking for work—friends of his own—and said that if anything could be found for us, he'd be very grateful. The man asked us where we were from and when we told him, he said, 'you're both very young but I'll see what I can do.'

O'Boyle left us there and said that he'd see us at knocking-off time. The man in the office told us to follow him and he ordered another man to get us two barrows.

'Now,' he said, 'come along here.'

Off we went and he brought the two of us to a part of the works where there was a heap of ore as high as Errigal.

'Now,' he said, 'if you want work, you can barrow that ore over to that furnace. You'll be paid ten shillings a week from Monday to Saturday. Think over it now but if you don't take it there's nothing more I can do for you.'

We looked at one another and made up our minds instantly to take the job. We took hold of the barrows. We hadn't arranged lodgings or anything else but we knew that O'Boyle wouldn't let us sleep out. When we knocked off, we met him and asked him if he had any address where we could try for lodgings. He said he had. He took us along with him and settled us with a woman from Annagry who kept lodgers. We were as well off as we could be then; we had work, a bit to eat and a bed of our own to stretch out on. I tell you, we didn't find making the bed too hard that night; and you can imagine our satisfaction as we stretched our bones in it—our first night in Scotland and our first day's pay earned as grown men making their own way.

We worked away shunting the ore but neither of us had any intention of staying in the works. We were waiting impatiently for the month of June. We knew that the men who came over thinning the turnips were expected in Berwickshire about the

twenty-second of that month. That was about the time they'd
be hoping to get work at the thinning. An odd year, it would
happen that the turnips wouldn't be ready by then and that
meant a week's hardship or more for the poor creatures while
they waited on work. Most of the work at home—of the heavy
work anyhow—would have been done by them before leaving.
Many crops would be saved and the turf cut. The women and
children would have to look after the rest while the men were
away. But there were women in our parish that would work
as well as any man and there was nothing that some of them
couldn't do—even to thatching a house.

FROM THE IRON-WORKS TO FARMING

As the middle of June came, we left the barrows and the iron
ore behind us and turned our faces towards the farmers. We
weren't in too great a hurry but we wanted to get up there
before the bulk of the men arrived from home. It wasn't the
same for us as for them with their knowledge of Scottish ways.
We forged ahead and we didn't know half the time whether
we were going astray or not. The weather was good and we
headed for Dunbar. It was to Edinburgh we wanted to go this
first time. We knew if we reached that town we wouldn't be
long covering the rest of the way. We knew from the talk we
heard at home that Haddington was about twenty-two miles
from Edinburgh and was on the way to Dunbar. Even if we
hadn't much English, we had tongues in our heads and we'd
find the way somehow.

Our feet were hardened a bit by now after the season spent
moving the ore but, even so, when we had walked a bit they
softened and got a bit scalded. We were ashamed to take off
our boots on this road. There were a lot of people on it and
it was as likely as not that we'd be attacked if we went barefoot.
So we kept our boots on.

There was hardly any real night at this time of the year and
whatever there was was as good as day—especially if you were
on the road. We kept on walking until well into the night.
Somewhere near Edinburgh we were when we came to the
edge of a wood.

'We might as well,' I said to Conal, 'go along in here and lay our heads down until morning.'

'That suits me,' said Conal, and you'd know from the way he said it that he was well satisfied that I had mentioned it. We lay down at the foot of a tree and little enough conversation passed between us as we fell asleep. I woke in the morning and, as I came to and looked around me, I felt just as if I had been drunk all night. This was the first night I had slept out but I can tell you it wasn't the last nor the most uncomfortable either. But since I wasn't used to it, I had enough aches as I woke up. There was nothing to be seen above me except the sky through the branches of the trees. I started up and jabbed at Conal with my elbow and told him to get up. He started rocking to and fro, stretching himself and drawing himself together, yawning and rolling and it's no lie or exaggeration to say that it was a quarter of an hour before he opened his eyes.

We made no delay in Edinburgh but we spent some time strolling about in Haddington when we reached there. We were hoping to meet someone from Cloghaneely there. There were plenty of men walking around and, indeed, some of them looked miserable enough. We knew by the look of them that they were on the 'tramp' the same as ourselves. It didn't look as if there was anyone among them from our parts and, when there wasn't, we took the road heading straight to the coast and Dunbar.

A fine country lay before us, neither a village nor a town on the way and nothing as far as the eye could see but lovely fine plains of the best land I have ever seen. You'd only see a homestead about every half-mile. Here and there was a big farmer's place with the cotters' houses and the labourers' huts lying near by it. I heard afterwards that there were holdings on this same road that had six thousand acres in them—some of them so big that it took the labourers forty minutes to walk from the house to the fields farthest away. The amount of land in these holdings was not counted by the number of acres any one contained but by the number of pairs of horses that would be working on the land. The man who had ten pairs working for him would be understood to have so many acres; the man who had twenty pairs would have twice as much land and so on.

BONNINGTON FARM

Some of our people worked for years at a place they called Bonnington Farm and as Conal and I drew near Dunbar we thought we'd go looking for that place. We did that and without much trouble indeed we found it. The holding wasn't as big as those around it. About six hundred acres it was in extent and unless my memory is failing me altogether I think that Young was the name of the man that owned it. He spoke to us nicely enough but whatever about the English on the Lagan, you wouldn't understand a word out of this man's mouth. We managed to let him know, however, what it was we wanted.

'Well,' he said (and I tell in my own words what I understood him to say). 'You're in luck. My turnips are ready for thinning any day now and I was just waiting for some of the people from your parts to come and start work on them. Come along with you now and I'll show you your quarters.'

Down we went with him. He unlocked the door and God himself would have taken a second look at what we saw in front of us. There was an old bed up in the corner of the hut with a few fistfuls of hay and a bit of rough sacking thrown on it. That was to be our bed. There were a few bits of coal in the other corner.

'I suppose now,' said the master to us, 'that you're a bit hungry now after your walk?'

'We are that,' we said both together.

'Fair enough,' he replied, 'I'll go up to the house now and bring you back something to eat. After that, you can look after yourselves.'

Off he went and it wasn't long until he came back with a bit of oatmeal and a couple of bowls and some milk.

'Now,' he said, 'you can mix the milk with the oatmeal and make some gruel. That will keep you going until you get something for yourselves. You can get out on the turnips tomorrow morning.'

He left us alone then.

We had never heard about this Scottish gruel beforehand. We had known of many other kinds of gruel that they made at home but we had never seen the cold oatmeal mixed with milk nor, now, had we any great desire to eat it. In our pockets we still had a couple of biscuits and we ate those with the cold milk. Then we started to look around us, we cleaned up the bothy as well as we could and made a bed of sorts for ourselves. Off we went then looking for a shop. We searched around until at last we found one a couple of miles from where we were. We bought some bread there and, after all, we had the master's word that we'd have plenty of milk in the house. Which we had.

We went to bed early that night. We were worn out and we knew that we'd have to be on our feet at the crack of dawn. And it was true. At six o'clock the following morning while we were still asleep, there was a loud knocking on the window and someone outside calling that it was time to be moving if we were going to do any work. We dressed quickly and having eaten a bit of bread to sop up the milk that we were given, out we moved. The bailiff was standing there waiting for us and he took us along to the field. And a fine field it was. Without any lie or exaggeration there must have been a hundred acres there under turnips. We were set at them. To be sure, we hadn't any experience of thinning but it wasn't hard to learn. Two shillings an acre was being paid for this work and I can tell you that young lads starting there would be a long time making their fortunes.

We worked away and it wasn't long until the people from Cloghaneely were arriving in hordes. In the place we were, only two men were needed until autumn. The first two who came got the work—James Gallagher and Micky Sweeney. The master knew them of an old date and, of course, we knew them also. The two of them are dead now this good number of years. James was about six feet six high and a droll fellow he was indeed. When he saw the old sacking on the bed, he became very critical and went straight up to the house to look for blankets; not only did he get one each for himself and his companion but he also got a couple of old ones for us. When he arose next morning, I asked him how he had slept.

'Sure, I didn't sleep at all,' he said.

'What was wrong with you?' I asked.

'O,' said he, 'my blanket was too short but when I come in tonight, I'll make it long enough.'

When the day was done and when we had come back in to the bothy, James sat down and had a smoke and a rest. After that, he went over to the bed and brought the blanket over by the fire. He took out a pocket-knife then and nicked the middle of the blanket. He seized it then and ripped it from top to toe. He had a needle and thread—as all the old hands who had been in Scotland before had. They usedn't have much clothes and when they'd tear them they'd have to be able to put a patch on them here and there. And they always had the necessary tools. James stitched the two pieces of blanket together anyhow and it was long enough for him that night.

CHANGE OF AIR AND OUTLOOK

We spent some time there (at Bonnington Farm) but neither Conal nor myself was very satisfied. James and Micky were used to hardship and they could put up with anything. They didn't care what they went through so long as they had the few pounds to bring home with them when the harvest was over. Some of the old people thought themselves very lucky if they made two pounds ten out of the harvest. But that was good money in those days. When a woman went to the shop, she could buy as much as she could carry for a shilling. But those days are gone.

Whatever about that, anyhow, Conal and myself thought that as the autumn drew near we wouldn't spend it where we were. We had the idea that we might move up to North Berwick. So we went, and whatever else could be said about the place, it was fine and healthy there beside the sea. We managed to get work on a holding out by the sea that suited us fine. There was a little bay there called County Bay and that great rock, Bass Rock, was right in the middle of it. I never went out to it for I was the kind of person all my life that got no pleasure from the sea, even boating if I could avoid it. They say that rock is about three hundred feet high and the sides are as steep as a gable from the top right down to the sea. I heard people say that there was only one particular place that you could land at on a quiet day on which the sea would not be anyway rough. There were lots of stories about the same rock and the Irish that were working thereabouts knew them all. I took a great interest in all this lore.

This was the last place in the three kingdoms that the soldiers stood to defend the Stuarts. There were only a dozen men left of King James's army; they fought every man that King William sent to take the Rock and they didn't let any man put his foot on it for three years. In the end, the food got scarce and they had to surrender. I heard also that, when the clergy were being persecuted, a lot of them were landed on the rock and that they were all left there without food or drink until they died.

We weren't thinking so much about that, I suppose, except that we had no particular desire to die of hunger. As the harvest came due, we started work. The only implement they had in this place was the scythe and even that was a step forward. It wasn't so long ago that throughout the whole of Scotland they were using only sickles. My elder brother who had been coming over for a few years beforehand had to bring his own sickle with him. But they were using scythes this first harvest I spent in North Berwick.

I thought the place I had just left at Bonnington was hard enough but here we hadn't even got bothies. We were working damned hard, sweating away in the fields all day; and when I'd come in at night-time, I'd have to lie down in the same place where the animals were tied up. Conal and myself had to lie down between two cows. To add to our troubles, the food we were getting wouldn't have kept a dog alive. As the harvest approached its end, we'd have to go out and do two hours work before we'd get a bite to eat at all. There'd be a kind of wild look in our eyes waiting for breakfast for we were dying with the hunger.

The master had a man with a gig who brought the stirabout out to the field. There was a small tub of stirabout to every five men. You had to go down on your knees and make a little hole in the stirabout into which you'd pour your milk. Out of fear, nobody would break the little divisions between the holes because, if he did, there'd be trouble and maybe whoever did it would get a skelp of a spoon across his gob. I wasn't a bit sorry when it ended and the time came to go home.

47

IV

The Land of Silver

THE 'CONVOY'

Five years altogether I spent going and coming between Scotland and Cloghaneely. The work was very hard over there—
from morning until midnight—though it wouldn't have
mattered so much if there had been any real return for it; but
the men who went over again and again at that time were no
better off for it. Nothing was thought of the Irish in Scotland
those days and as well as every other ill-usage they received,
they certainly weren't paid in any way commensurate with the
work they did. The food was very bad too and as we ourselves
knew to our cost even the beds that they had to stretch out on
weren't by any means good. I was getting pretty well fed up
with the way I was living. Sometime beforehand some relatives
of mine had gone over to America and they wrote and told us
that it was a much better country than Scotland. I spoke to
Conal Eileen one night about this and confided in him—that
I was thinking of going to America.

'Well,' said Conal, 'do what you think best. I've no
intention of crossing over there. You've often heard the old
saying that the far-off hills are green and maybe you shouldn't
build too much on emigrating.'

'Maybe you're right,' I said, 'but whatever comes of it, I'm
going, with the help of God, to have a look at it.'

48

THE 'CONVOY'

It wasn't hard to get to America at that time. You only had to go to Derry and get on the boat—so long as you had the money there was no trouble about it. A relative of mine, Francis Ferry, was working in the iron-works at Bethlehem, Northampton County, Pennsylvania; I wrote to him and told him what I was thinking of doing. He wrote back to me straight away and said that I'd be welcome if I thought that I'd do better there than in Scotland. I started getting ready to go then and I need hardly tell you that there was a sight of difference between going to Scotland and going to New York.

It was the custom at that time that anyone going to America would walk around the village for a day or two before he left. He would have to shake hands with old and young, big and small. There would be laments in every house and blessings galore would be called down on the person who was on his way. As night fell, most of the people of the district would gather into the 'convoy-house'—the old people in the first instance up to ten o'clock and then the young people. There'd be drinking and music and dancing then until morning. The person leaving would be keened* three times altogether during the night. Often some of the men would be the worse for drink because it was the custom to send the hat around early on and have a little collection. Whiskey and potheen were cheap and plentiful and threepence or fourpence a head would suffice to give a big night for the whole company. If a fiddler was to be had without much trouble, well, he was there; if not, there were always people who would keep the dancing going until morning by lilting. Sometimes the women would bring in chickens and bread; but there would always be food and drink without it costing the emigrant's family a penny.

With the first streak of daylight, the real lamentation would start. The person who would be about to set out on the long road would be drowned with tears and dried with kisses and the whole gathering would accompany him three or four miles along the beginning of the journey. Then they'd stand until the emigrant was well out of sight. It wasn't to be wondered at, of course, as often enough that would be the last sight of him a lot of them would ever have.

*Lamented.

49

Three of us were going together, myself and a couple of relations: Tom Ferry, a brother of the man already over there and Jimmy Doherty (or Jimmy Anthony as we called him) who lived practically next door to me. It was the month of May and the weather was grand. We arranged to gather together in my house at early morning and to leave as soon as we could. Neither I nor anybody else in the house got a wink of sleep that night. We had a lot to talk over and the night was far too short for us.

Well, the time came. Jimmy and his people were already in our house and we were waiting for Tom's people. It wasn't the noise of footsteps that we first heard approaching the house but a kind of sobbing—someone who had been lamenting so much that he had lost his breath. They all came in—Tom and his people—but they had hardly time to sit down. It was almost daybreak and we had to have Muckish Gap behind us before people were on the road or there'd be more neighbours coming along to delay us further. But the real sadness came when it was time to say goodbye to our own people. Well, it was hard to say the words but we did and then we were on our way. Conal Eileen strode along as well as anyone and he came with me as far as Gortahork where he said his final parting words. Little I thought that morning that would be the last sight I'd ever have of him. The poor lad was buried before I returned and I was heart-broken when I heard he had died.

Walking was the only means of travelling then and those going to America had to foot-slog it as far as Derry. It's about thirty miles from our place to Letterkenny through Muckish Gap and twenty miles further to Derry. We had to cover those fifty miles by evening in order to make the boat. During the summertime a lot of people would go to Tory instead of to Derry. At Tory, they could transfer from a lobster boat on to the ship at high tide; but unless the weather was very good, maybe two ships would pass on their way to America before a person could get on in this fashion. For this reason, most people —like ourselves—preferred to go to Derry. We had no anxiety about making Derry in time. We were well used to walking and we had hardly any baggage. When we arrived, we went and got something to eat and after that we didn't care where the sun shone on us. All we had to do was to pay the passage-money in the office of the ship we intended to take. Four pounds ten shillings each we paid and then we were ready to go aboard.

ON BOARD THE BOAT

The ship was due to sail at six o'clock in the evening. There were hundreds boarding her as well as ourselves. The vessel cast off and we moved slowly down Lough Foyle. It was a beautiful evening and the bay was as still as a sheet; but, if it was, it was nothing to the stillness on board. There was nothing to be heard except the creaking of the ropes as the sailors pulled them here and there and an occasional shout from the pilot as he guided us on our way. Save for women and children, few went below deck until we moved out beyond the mouth of the Lough—soon enough we'd see the last of our native land. When we got outside, there was a high north-easterly wind with the tide running against it so that the sea was rising and turning as if it was being churned. Our little group were all together and Jimmy Anthony was standing beside me with his arm across my shoulder for support. Like myself, his sea-legs weren't of the best. He was looking at the sky between himself and the horizon and shortly, I saw him bending his head as he used to do when something was worrying him.

'There's something in the sky over there,' he said, 'that I don't like.'

'I never saw you any other way,' I said, 'what's wrong with the sky?'

'There's nothing wrong with the sky,' he answered, 'but look at those "feet" sticking up from the sun there at the edge. There's nothing so unnatural as "feet" sticking up.'

'Well, I won't say you're not right,' I said.

'It will be easy enough now for three or four days,' he said, 'but there's a lot of violence there and it's often enough it is as late as this in the year. This is the "May Screech" and maybe it's late coming this year. It's the fury of this storm that kills the old cows for want of forage.'

With that, the vessel turned around by Malin Head and, as it turned, it took a lot of water aft. The people then weren't slow at getting below deck. I wasn't the last man to get below and once I got there I stayed there.

I told you before that there wasn't a worse sailor in the whole world than myself; but however I managed on the journeys to Scotland, the spasms I had were only trotting after what I suffered when we were less than an hour out of Lough Foyle. Even before we reached Tory Island, I would have been quite happy for my companions to grab me and toss me overboard and have done with it. My heart was in my mouth thinking that I had ten or eleven days of this to go through— that is, if I lived at all. The people aboard were as nice and kind to me as anyone could be but, the state I was in, I couldn't have cared less about their kindness. Now and again, a steward would come over to me with a drop of brandy and, if it hadn't been for that, I never would have seen land or sea again.

After putting over three or four days of that, I came to myself and it was as if I had lost all memory of what life was like, while I was down. I started to look around me and what I saw was rough enough. About ten of us were thrown together in a little cabin no bigger than the cabin on the boat to Scotland. On two sides of the cabin, there were wooden benches that were as hard as rocks. There was nothing soft about our beds either and there was hardly enough clothes on them that would cover a corpse on a shutter. When we'd feel like eating, the food put down before us wasn't any too palatable—a few sea-biscuits that were as hard as a ram's horn, a drop of tea, or of coffee the colour of which was so dirty that it reminded me of the colour of the flood-water in Glenna River as it raced down after a long spell of drought. The taste of the biscuits upset my stomach but there were one or two among us that had brought a few oatmeal cakes with them from home. It was on the few odd mouthfuls of those we survived until we got across.

On the eleventh day, it was announced that we were coming near New York. I gathered myself together, as they say, I moved around a bit. I was as weak as water-gruel, but at least

I was alive. But what other way could I be, seeing that the last proper bite of food I had had was before we left Derry.

NEW YORK AND BETHLEHEM

It's strange how things run through a person's head at times. I always thought that it was little I had learned at school in Magheraroarty. In spite of that, however, I understood the English language better the last couple of seasons than I did when I started out. I began, too, to get an interest in poetry. I liked when the master would read aloud a poem that we understood and when he'd make us learn bits of it off by heart. He worked hard enough trying to teach us other things as well but I forgot everything except the Catechism and the few bits of poetry. I saw a lot in my life since then that reminded me of that poetry and that would make me say to myself that the poet who wrote it was very perceptive. It was like that as I gazed wide-eyed at New York for the first time. I recalled immediately a little poem by Wordsworth that was in our Third Book where he spoke of morning in a city:

> Earth has not anything to show more fair:
> Dull would he be of soul who could pass by
> A sight so touching in its majesty.

But I had little chance to engage in poetic vein about New York—or about anywhere else in America. I still had a hundred miles to go to reach Frank Ferry in Bethlehem, Pennsylvania. We didn't want to delay at all in New York for we knew that as soon as we got to where he was, we could take our ease for he'd look after us. I had a little bit of money as I hadn't spent a red cent on the boat there being nothing to spend it on until we landed. I had enough to ensure that we'd be alright for a couple of days if we remained in New York but we knew that the rest would do us much more good if we waited for the end of the journey.

We finally got to Bethlehem and there was Frank waiting for us at the railway station. I didn't know him all that well for I was only a very young boy when he left home but he

53

recognized us and as soon as he saw us getting off the train he came and spoke to us.

Bethlehem is divided into two parts—North Bethlehem and South Bethlehem. It was in South Bethlehem that Frank lived. There was a large iron and steel works there. There was a river known as the river Lehigh running through the city and on the north side of it there lay flour-mills, silk and textile factories and dye-works. A lot of people were coming into this city and like every other city similarly situated the biggest difficulty was to find houses for the people to live in. A lot of Irishmen came there. Houses and factories were going up rapidly and there was plenty of work, if heavy itself, for anybody that had a mind for it.

Frank brought us along and fixed us up with lodgings. He put me in with a quiet married couple named Cannon from Cloghaneely. The man of the house had lost his health in the iron-works and his wife and daughters were hard enough put to it to make ends meet and keep themselves alive. The poor woman would be running around the house looking after those of us who were staying there and she hadn't a shoe on her foot —nor had her daughters—no more than if they were all back there in Cloghaneely itself. She was very good to me though, I can say that.

When I found myself among my own people there in Bethlehem, I thought I'd take a bit of a rest. I spent a week wandering around gazing at all the wonders and at the surrounding country. Mind you, it wasn't all that big a city in those days but industry was growing rapidly there. That was the reason why the trains called there. You'd never see a bus or a motor car there then nor, indeed, for a long time afterwards. There was a big town about five miles away called Easton. It was there the church was and the big shops and, if we were needing anything, we had to go there to get whatever it was. Enormous coal-trains went to Easton and they were so long that they had to go very slowly. We would attach ourselves to one of these and in that way we'd get to Easton without paying a penny for we hadn't much money in our pockets then. We had friends down there with whom we'd spend a good night now and again.

THE CONNAUGHTMAN THAT I FLATTENED

At the end of the week, I sailed out looking for work. There were large boats bringing sand up the Lehigh to be used building the houses and the first job I got was unloading these boats. The boat would be tied up there on the river with a plank leading from it on to the bank. The sand would be taken out in barrows along this plank. I got a barrow and started work; the pay was one dollar a day.

THE CONNAUGHTMAN THAT I FLATTENED

There was a lot of Irishmen working on these boats as well as myself and in the boat that I was helping to unload, there was a Connaughtman who had been over a good while and who was very knowledgeable about the work. I was nervous enough, to tell you the truth, going in and out on that narrow plank with a heavy barrow. If I got upset or dizzy or anything like that and fell this way or that way, I'd be straight into the river and in danger of drowning for I hardly knew how to swim. This Connaughtman saw that I was very nervous and he started jeering me. All the Connaughtmen I met over there were very much given to this game. Well, the jeering went on for a long time but though it upset me a good deal, I didn't say anything. I thought to myself, however, that I wouldn't stand it much longer and that I'd be dug out of him before I was much older. I waited my opportunity for a few days and at last I met him coming off while I was going on the boat. I lifted my fist and struck him on the ear throwing himself and his barrow into the river where he sank to the bottom.

The Connaughtmen used to call the people from our county who were over there, the 'Far-downs' but when I slung that fellow in the river, I tell you he was 'far-down'. I thought he was well dealt with; and though I expected to be half-killed, nobody said a word to me. It wasn't long until he surfaced and a couple of his friends grabbed him and pulled him out of the river. Because he was drowned wet, he had to go off home and I didn't get a sight of him for a long time afterwards. He came back to work but, if he did, he didn't come on the boat where I was working. He was too much afraid of me.

I worked away there but the pay was small and we had to

work ten hours a day for it. I decided I'd leave and get a job in the iron-works. I went up there. I knew a few men who were working there and they got me taken on.

Work never stopped in that place at any time. Always on Saturday, a whole twenty-four hour shift had to be put in and, as the men who had been working all the week were worn out, some of them didn't work those long hours on Saturday. The management of the works would then get in some of the men unloading sand to give a hand. One Saturday, they sent out for a roster and who do you think was put working with me but the very same man that I had dealt the treacherous blow to and had slung in the river. I was nervous enough when I saw him coming towards me but I wouldn't give him the satisfaction of letting him see that. When he came over, I spoke to him as roughly as if I was a foreman in the place:

'Bend to it.' I said. 'Get off your coat and do something. I'll make you sweat now.' He didn't answer 'yes, aye or no' and never spoke to me from that day forward. He was always telling other men that he would do for me but he was too frightened of me to do anything about it.

WE LEAVE THE BIG TOWNS

I worked in Bethlehem for a year and I can tell you that, between hard work and low pay, I thought no more of America than I did of Scotland. Everyone that you met was trying to get more out of you than the next person and bad as life was in Scotland, it wasn't much better in America. The old hands who had worked Scotland for many a long day were of the opinion that the availability of work there was no longer what it had been and that soon there would be no jobs there for anybody. Be that as it may, we thought longingly of Scotland after we'd been a while beyond.

We all resolved that we wouldn't stay very long where we were but that we'd collect a bit of money and see more of the country. My friend, Jimmy Doherty, and I decided that one of us would go out to one of the western states where they were mining for silver and that the other man would stay back; that whoever would go would get the money we had saved; and that if he didn't make out, money would be sent to enable him to return. We drew lots—long and short straws—to see which of us would go and the choice fell on Jimmy. We made our farewells in due course and Jimmy set off, the poor fellow, not knowing what lay in store for him. But he was a shrewd young man well able to stand up for himself with any man, black, white or yellow, in America.

I had to wait a long time for news from him but in the end, after about six months, I got a letter. He told me to get myself together and follow him out as quickly as I could to some remote part of Montana.

Shortly after we got to Bethlehem, my friend, Tom Ferry left us and went down to a little town called Norristown about forty miles south. I didn't like to leave for the 'wild west' without looking him up so the Sunday before I left, I went down by train to Norristown. I had his address and I found him without very much trouble. I gave him the news and when he heard what it was, he said that he too was getting a bit fed up with the place he was in. Nothing would do him then except to accompany me. While the idea of having company was nice and cheering, I would have preferred him to stay where he was as I hadn't any inkling as to what might happen at the end of the journey. But it was no good my pointing this out to him and in the end I told him to do whatever he wished. We fixed the day and other matters and Tom said that he'd be at the railway station in Allentown (I think that was the venue) on the day of my departure. I left it like that and returned home in the evening. I told the couple I was staying with that I intended to leave. They were very sad at this and tried to persuade me to remain. If I had known what was before me, maybe I would have. But, as they say, God gave no faculty of foresight even to His Mother; and maybe, all things considered, it's just as well that none of us have that gift.

As the day of departure arrived, I had everything ready; I bade farewell to the people of the house and made off towards the station. I left Anna, the daughter of the house—a little girl about sixteen or seventeen—working away in the house and no more of a boot or a stocking on her than she ever had. I took my time getting to the station. I was sitting there in the carriage not thinking about anything in particular when what happened but that little devil of a daughter of the house that I had left working with her mother got into the carriage and sat down right in front of me. I don't have to tell you that the sight of that girl there bowled me over, altogether. Just then, the whistle blew and the train pulled out before I had time to ask her what mischief she was up to. The train was out of the station before I understood rightly what was in her mind. 'I'm tired of the way I am,' she said, 'and I was hoping that you'd pay my fare to wherever you're heading for. I might get a bit of work to do there that'd pay me something.'

'Well, devil the foot you're going with me,' I said. 'I've enough to do to get myself out there and not knowing what's in store for me when I get there. As soon as the train stops, you'll have to get out and go right back straight away to your people.'

I knew the train would stop where Tom would be waiting for me. When it did, I managed to send the girl off and I put her on a train to take her back to where we had come from. I wandered idly around for a while until the train arrived that Tom was to be on. It came and he was on it and we were ready to set out. We had no call to buy food on the train for the woman I lodged with had readied a big basket of food—meat and bread—for me before I left and there was so much in the basket that it kept us going most of the way.

The journey took us six days. Any time we had the chance to get a lift free—on a coal truck or suchlike—we took it. Otherwise, we bought tickets. Neither of us lay down on a bed during the whole period. We could have got beds on the trains if we had had any money but that commodity was scarce with us so we had to sit up on the carriage seats. Even that was better, however, than an uncomfortable and illegal ride in a goods truck. But even when we were paying our way, I was afraid to put my head down and get a wink of sleep for fear that the little basket of food I had would be stolen and that I'd be left without anything at all. It wasn't safe to sleep on the trains then for a lot of the kind of people that travelled on them thought no more of killing a human than they thought of killing a midge. Scores were being murdered on the trains in

58

those days, particularly those that looked as if they had something in their pockets. Our pockets weren't all that heavy but,
even so, we had to keep our eyes well open.

We crossed over the great wide plains of America until we
came to the mountains and the city of Missoula. We got a
smaller, narrower train there that took us further into the
hills. Trains didn't go past a certain point so we walked the last
five miles up a mountain path until we got to the end of our road.

MINING IN MONTANA

Montana is one of the biggest states in America. It lies in the
north-west of the country by the borders of Canada and I'd
estimate that it's about three times the size of Ireland. It was a
very remote place, the time I was there. The part of Montana
I was in was right in the heart of the Rocky Mountains in the
western areas of the state. It was a very remote and inaccessible
place, the time I was there. Few white people lived in these
areas other than those in the mining camps; there were no
trains or indeed any way of travelling except by horse back or
by foot—and horses were few and far between. There was no
road there other than a narrow little path marked out by the
Indians centuries before we got there. People walking there in
winter had to walk one after the other just like the Tory
islanders had to do coming up from their boats. No two could
walk side by side for the snow was so heavy in places that they had
to keep rigidly to the beaten path. 'Trails', they called such paths.

About fifty miles east of Missoula, there were a couple of
silver mines in the mountain called Granite Mountain. This is
about 7,000 feet high and is as tough as its name implies. It
was in one of those mines that my friend Jimmy Doherty was
working—the lad who sent for me and first asked me to come
out. But when I went out, I couldn't get work in the 'Granite'
mines. I took it easy for a week then, after which I got a job
about five miles further on in the hills where they were building
huge furnaces to 'run' or melt the silver, in. An Irishman named
Cosgrave was my foreman on the building job there. He was a
kind gentle man and I was satisfied enough with myself.

I worked away there as hard as I could until Christmas

came. Frost and snow, the like of which I had never seen before, fell. The cold was so bad that I had to get back to Granite Mountain even though the chances were that there wouldn't be any work for me there. That was where my friends and those I knew were—men from Cloghaneely and distantly related to me. I think I was a bit unhappy in the other place as well, among people who spoke only English and other foreign languages, and it was that more than anything else that drove me back to the mines.

After Christmas, one of the men I knew managed to get me a job in one of the 'Granite' silver mines. In this job, I'd have to work underground. I knew nothing at all about work of this kind and I didn't know what was in front of me. The first time I went down the shaft, I had to walk a mile and a half from the place where I entered. Two miners were working there all day with a mechanical drill and at the end of the day they would put charges in the holes and detonate them. A heap of stones and clay would be left. I had to get into these holes on a night shift and put the stones and earth on a little car to be taken out. At the beginning, my heart was up in my mouth with fear. I thought of the length of time I was underground, the huge mountain over me and how little lay between me and eternity; and I didn't feel at all too satisfied. But as the old saying has it, there I was and there I'd stay and I had to put up with it. After a while I got so used to the work that I wasn't conscious of the danger at all. I used to go down the mine as confidently as I'd go for a pail of water at home.

I worked hard there and honestly for the foreman who was over me. He was quite satisfied with me, as I was with him. He was a small-sized Englishman and I seldom worked under a man as honest and as decent.

When I had been four years on that work, he asked me if I'd like to learn to be a miner. He said if I had any wish for it, he'd give me a good chance because I had stayed so long and had given him such good service. He left me to think about it and gave me a couple of days to make up my mind. Then he asked me for my decision. I told him that undoubtedly I'd like to learn the trade because I didn't think it would be any burden on me whatever I did later. As well as that, I was thinking that if it ever came to pass that I could buy a bit of land for myself, it would be good to know as much as I could about mining. I fixed up, therefore, to learn the trade. I was put to work with a little Englishman who was advanced enough in years and I spent four months with him. I learned the trade well then—everything to do with mining; the kind of rock that would be carrying the silver; the way to break it and explode it ; how to load and send it on its way; the best way to get at the silver and to get it out of the rocks; the handling of the drills; how to use props and beams to keep the roofs and walls safely up and so forth. Of course, I had a fair amount of knowledge about the work already because of the length of time I had spent below with the miners and the other workers; that meant the trade was a bit easier for me to take in.

All the time that I was learning about the different aspects of mining, I was getting direction and advice and a knowledge of the craft from that old Englishman I mentioned but when my time was up I had to get out working on my own. Everyone was very good to me, however, and during that four months the boss paid me the same wages that he was paying to those who had known the trade for years. Seven years all told I spent in the silver mines, getting better and more knowledgeable with every day that passed.

THE INDIANS AND THE KIDNAPPED WOMAN

The part of Montana I found myself in was as rough as you'd get anywhere. Huge barren hills surrounded the place where we worked—nothing to be seen on them from foot to peak but massive rugged rocks everywhere. There wasn't a sight of grass, sedge or heather anywhere and, indeed, you'd hardly be surprised at that seeing that, for the most of the year, they were covered with ice and snow. The only way to get to the mine was to climb by a narrow path that ran up the slope of the mountain. Once a week or so, four horses would haul a load of food and drink up the path from the wide valley that lay at the foot of the mountain. And, apart from the teams that took the silver away from the mine, we had no other contact with the great world outside.

The valley below us was inhabited by Red Indians and strong rugged-featured men they were, too. I'm told they gave its name to the river that was below us for it was called the Great Blackfoot River. There was a tribe of the 'Blackfeet' away north of us in Montana and there was another crowd called 'Flatheads' away west of them again. A lot of Jesuits worked among these Indians at one time and were very good to them until one day the soldiers came and attacked the Indians and then, of course, it was like putting the match to the fuse again. Many of the mission stations were named out of Jesuit hagiography—I heard of towns near enough to us named St. Ignatius and De Smet (after Father De Smet).

Whenever the hunt was on for the Indians, they'd flee to these lonely valleys like the one down below us and settle in them for a few years. There they'd work the rough earth and, in a few years, would have turned it into rich arable land. They were good marksmen by this time and would kill a lot of wild animals—buffalo, moose and the like—and that's what kept life in them. But as the white man advanced, the wild animals were getting scarcer and life was getting more difficult for the Indians and their women and children. They all had large families and it was hard to look after them.

Their 'squaws' would come down to our cabins leading mules carrying baskets holding five or six children. Their men were able to make the baskets so that they fitted snugly on to the mules. I often saw these squaws coming to us with six children carried that way.

They'd walk around from cabin to cabin and every bit of the waste food we'd have thrown out—pieces of bread, meat and that sort—they'd gather and take back with them down the valley. Some days they'd have a basket full of this waste as they returned. It was very seldom that the men would come up to us. They were afraid enough and if they came at all it would be during the night. We, in our turn, were frightened enough any night we heard them moving about outside. They were dangerous and if they got into your cabin they'd no more worry about killing you than they'd worry about killing a beetle.

There were a lot of white people from different countries living in a place called Greenough up on the shoulder of the mountain near us and the Indians would go there from time to time and try to kidnap the women and the girls. The women would have to be always on the watch and not stir outside their own doors unless they had their men-folk or some other men to accompany them; and even the men wouldn't go out without plenty of firearms with them.

A man from Cloghaneely—one of the O'Donnells—was out there at the same time as myself and he had a fine comely wife with him. They hadn't been very long in the place and didn't give any kind of thought to danger. He went off about his business one day, leaving her behind him in the cabin. It would seem that one of the red bucks laid his eye on her at some stage and he lay in wait until he saw the husband going off. When the coast was clear, up he came and bore her off with him. Some of his own people were waiting for him at the edge of the wood beside the town and, throwing her across a horse's back, off they made down the valley.

When the man returned in the evening, there was neither sight nor sound to be had of his wife nor any sign that any housework had been done since morning. The poor man was nearly out of his mind and, when he went searching for her among the other cabins, it was clear to the old hands that one of the red men had kidnapped her. Their anger mounted and all the men in the place gathered together with their guns and set off down the valley looking for her. They intended to wreak havoc and desolation on the Red Indians if they didn't find her.

Luckily enough, there was no fighting. As they came to the Indian camp, they saw the woman they were looking for sitting among a crowd at the door of one of the cabins; and as soon as the Indians saw the menacing crowd coming towards them with their arms at the ready, off they made like rabbits, leaving her behind them. Her man took her up and brought her back to their own cabin. The poor creature was so frightened by her experience that she wouldn't let her man go out to work any more and, in the end, they left the district altogether. The miners around the place helped them generously while they were waiting to leave. They made a collection for them and the pair went back to civilized parts. At the same time, the poor woman never did any good from then until she died. Her heart had been frightened out of her although the Indians hadn't harmed her at all.

I was one of the band that helped to rescue that woman and I didn't care whether or not I was shot so long as we got her out of the hands of those red devils. At the same time, it was no wonder the Indians were the way they were. There was neither peace nor comfort for them anywhere. They'd come to a little valley, like what I told you about, and build little wooden houses for themselves. Then they'd start work on the rough ground around them until they'd turn it into a fine rich field stretching as far as the eye could see. As soon as the American authorities would hear about this, they'd send a large army from the civilized part of America to drive these poor people further into the remotest reaches of the hills. Often the soldiers had to fight a hard battle before scattering them and sometimes a second and a third battle would have to be fought before the Indians would be defeated and routed. They'd hold out bravely trying to keep the bit of land they'd worked so hard for but, in the end, the superiority of men and weapons would tell and they'd have to retreat away back into the mountains. Some greedy white man—someone with friends at court or a planter without any conscience—would then get the land for himself. Hundreds of battles between the red men and the white men were fought in the countryside around where we were and I often heard talk about 'Custer's Last Stand' and about the whole war against the Sioux that had taken place about twenty years previously. Much of the fighting took place down by Bitter-Root River and that wasn't very far away from us.

The Indians that were left here and there were in a bad way and we had a great deal of pity for them—the same thing had happened to ourselves home in Ireland. We knew their plight well. We understood their attachment to the land of their ancestors and their desire to cultivate it as well as their wish to keep their own customs and habits without interference from the white man. We were interfering with them, I suppose, as well as everybody else but at least some of us sensed that if they were wild itself, it was not without cause.

BUILDING A HOUSE

Five or six of us from Donegal were working together in the silver mines of Granite Mountain. When we were well settled in and had got to know the people fairly well, we thought we ought to build a little cabin for ourselves instead of paying out rent as we had been doing so far. Little wooden cabins were all that the place contained and the building of one wasn't likely to take us very long. There was a forest beside us with the best of wood—yew and spruce and other kinds—growing in it. All we had to do was to go out with an axe—which we did—and in a few days, we felled enough trees to build a castle let alone a small cabin. We brought them in, cut them into logs and left them ready to be assembled.

It took us a couple of days to build the house and it wouldn't have taken that length of time except that a couple of us had to go into Greenough, the town nearest us, to get nails and bolts. When they came back, we were no time finishing the job. We got the skeleton up and then everyone was able to drive in bolts and nails and get the planks together so as to make a roof. We fixed more planks above those and we were all sorry that we hadn't any thatch so that we could make it look more like home. But there was fine clay to be had around about and, when you worked it with a shovel, it was as good as any cement you could get anywhere. We worked up a good amount of this clay and put it on top of the planks. When that settled and froze, it was like slate and it never let any moisture through.

UNEMPLOYMENT

Seven years we spent in that cabin and we hadn't a bit of trouble as long as we were there. We had plenty of food and were saving a good bit of money and it looked as if we'd never leave the place. But nothing lasts for ever and it was like that with us. We were working silver all the time and the demand for it was uncertain enough in America at that time. There were debates about 'Bimetallism' and 'Free Silver' and about the proper value of gold as compared with silver and so on. I never understood the matter very well at any time but I remember that people who owned silver mines used get grants but Grover Cleveland put a stop to that when he became President. Things like that would happen from time to time. According to whether the government favoured the 'Free Silver' people or didn't—or as affairs of state went this way or that—the value of silver would change. I remember there was a bad time about 1896 and the value fell. It was worth eighty-five cents an ounce when we started working at it but later, in the twinkling of an eye, it fell to forty cents. Some of the mines—our own included—had to be closed as the owners were unable to meet the overheads and pay the men. They kept the married men on but the younger people that were there had to take to the roads.

There were five or six of us young fellows together—all of us related in one way or another—and when we were sacked from the mine, we didn't know where we'd turn to look for work. We knew well enough that it was no good staying where we were as long as the value of silver was what it was. If we stayed on hoping for a change in the situation, we'd more than likely run through every penny we had. We'd be cleaned out completely—worse off than we ever had been and not a chance that there would be anyone to look after us.

THE BASE GOLD OF MONTANA

In the end, we thought the best thing we could do would be to make for the hills even further west and look for something for ourselves there. It wouldn't have done to have gone back east with nothing to boast about since we left there. We knew that gold had been found in several places in Montana before that. We had heard tell of the fortunes that had been made in Grasshopper Creek, where the city of Bannock now stands and at Last Chance Gulch where Helena, the state capital, was built. But we knew that there was gold nearer to Granite Mountain than that. Some of the men working in the silver

mines talked about places like Goldcreek and Pioneer and
Lone Tree Hill in the mountains to the south and we thought
that we might do a bit of prospecting as well as anyone else.
We were a fine robust bunch of lads and young to boot. The
country itself, indeed, was young. It wasn't as developed and
industrialised as it is now. Gold, silver, copper and other
minerals were plentiful. Anybody that wanted to could get
rich there. As for us, we had nothing to lose and everything to
gain. And if we struck gold, never a poor day would we see
again as long as we lived.

We made ready—seven of us—at the beginning of the
summer; each of us had a large pack with provisions of all
kinds including flour, bacon, coffee and sugar. We also had
mining gear and various other tools with us: pick-axes, shovels,
crowbars and such-like; and we headed out for the desolate
mountains around Mount Baldy. There, we moved east, west
and south in our search for gold. We hadn't the implements to
go down deep so our searches were confined to the surface: all
we could engage in was what they called 'placer mining'. We'd
dig an odd hole here and there and hope to come across something. The places we'd choose would always be by a stream or
a running brook that would wash the clay and the gravel
away. If we were lucky, some day the sieveing we had to do
would result in a piece of gold being left in the 'pan' and we'd
know that we were in the right place.

We dug a lot of holes like this before we came across anything. At last, we came to a little river where the water had a
yellow tinge; we took this to be a good sign, an indication that
there was gold-dust in it. There may have been some little
nuggets in the stream itself but whether it was that we didn't
think of it at the time or that we were avaricious, we decided
to look for the vein itself in the overhanging hills. Anyway, we
selected one of the hills and sunk a shaft near the top. Down
we dug through the clay and the gravel for about twenty feet
before we struck rock. There was a trace of gold in the rock
right enough, but it was hardly worth mentioning. At the same
time, we thought it might be worth our while to tunnel into
the side of the hill until we joined with the hole we had dug
down through the top.

We weren't too well equipped for the work and we were too far from the big town to fetch the tools we needed. The first thing we did, therefore, after digging the hole down from the top of the hill was to make a small forge just where we intended to start the tunnel. One of us—Tom Ferry—was a kind of blacksmith and he was able to forge the drills, the picks and the wedges for us. That was Tom's job—that and cooking for us—and I can tell you he was as good a cook as you'd get. Apart from him, there were six of us, and each pair took it in turns to do the work—eight hours for every pair. We laboured incredibly hard opening that tunnel, nearly killing ourselves now we were working on our own. I don't believe that any workers ever abused themselves as we did then and that's why we were hoping that, if ever we struck what was in the top of the hill, we'd have no more worries for the rest of our lives.

One night, myself and Jimmy Doherty were working on the night shift. As usual, we made a couple of holes and then, about ten o'clock, returned to the cabin for a bite of supper. When we finished, we went back to the holes and exploded the charges. With the explosion, we were sure our fortunes were made. We could see, by the light of the candles we had brought with us, the shine of the gold! This was the vein, without any doubt. We wrung one another's hands and could hardly restrain ourselves from wakening our comrades up to tell them.

We picked up what had been loosened from the rock and took a load each down to where the cabin was. We wakened the other five and showed them what we had. As soon as they saw the nuggets, they too were sure that our fortunes were made. By this, it was after midnight. They got up out of bed, flung on their clothes and I'm telling you we had a night's celebration on account of it. We had a few drops of spirits and, naturally, the gold would bring us no luck unless we drowned it properly first. There wasn't a drop in the cabin that we didn't drink!

We knew rightly ourselves that it was real gold we had struck but, just to be on the safe side, and to make assurance doubly sure, next morning we sent one of the boys down south to a little town called Phillipsburg to determine exactly what wealth we had. We drew lots for this and it fell to Owen

MacNeelish from Gweedore to make the journey. It was in the depths of winter and we were up to our knees in snow and frost. We were all wearing Norwegian snow-shoes for without them we couldn't have ventured out at all. Next morning, Owen donned a pair of these and set off walking through the snow. He carried with him three or four small bags containing samples of the mineral we had come across. Phillipsburg was about fifty miles away and it would take him three or four days to reach it and to find a man who could tell him what it was worth.

When he left, the six of us that remained went into the cave in the side of the hill and started to work like mad to get out as much of the mineral as we could. Something over a week went by and we had blasted a lot of the rock and taken out a good deal of gold, as we thought. But back Owen arrived and one look at him told us that everything was not all that right. The news he returned with was that the gold we had found was not worth very much. It was too rough, too dark and it wouldn't pay us at all to work the place unless there was finer gold there. Our hearts sank altogether and we were left without a word to throw among ourselves. We weren't too satisfied after all our work and the way we had driven ourselves; but it couldn't be helped and complaining about it didn't get us anywhere.

At the same time, we had a lot to complain about. We were out in the backwoods and not too sure at all where exactly we were; there were ramparts of snow all around us and the cold was getting in on us for the cabin wasn't as good as the one we had had at Granite Mountain; but the worst of it all was that we hadn't enough food to see us through the winter. We'd have to get out of the place before long—it would be senseless to stay there—but where on earth would we turn our faces to? We talked the whole thing over and were all agreed that it would be best to stay as we were until the days stretched a bit coming near St. Patrick's Day. We had a bit of money left for we hadn't spent foolishly while we were at Granite Mountain and we had spent even less since leaving there; we'd get something, however little, for the gold we had gathered and one or two of us could make their way into one of the big towns and bring us up some food.

St. Patrick's Day wasn't too far away. Irishmen who are in America make a great day out of this; they are neither slow nor ashamed to admit that they are Irish and they all go out celebrating the day in a proper fashion. In that year 1897, as the great day approached, we decided to return to where we had come from—Granite Mountain—and with the help of God to spend the feast there.

And we did that. We came in and met all those we knew who were still there and had a great time—food and drink, music and companionship. In the crowd, we met a little man from Cork named MacCarthy—a man we knew well when we had been there before. He had stayed in Granite Mountain during all that time of unemployment and he had nothing to show for it. He was a fine young fellow and didn't know, no more than ourselves, where he would go. As we got friendly together again, we had long chats about what would be best for us to do. He had fine education, this man from Cork— something that a lot of people out there at that time hadn't got—and he told us about the newspaper accounts of the nugget of gold that people had found up in the Klondike the previous summer. That was the first time I heard the magic word 'Klondike' but I can tell you it wasn't the last time. Myself and my fate were interwoven with it for a long while afterwards.

V

Between Two Lands

RUMOURS OF GOLD

Michael MacCarthy had a wonderful story for us on the St. Patrick's Day of that year 1897. Some man named Carmac had found a nugget of gold the previous summer in the icy region of north-west Canada. There were plenty of stories in the papers about it, MacCarthy told us. People in the big towns along the coast of America—places like Seattle and Portland—were talking of going there as quickly as they could. Those who were up in Klondike already were writing letters to their relatives about the wealth they had got and something of what they were saying was being published in local newspapers. MacCarthy told us this at Granite Mountain; we started to talk of going to Klondike ourselves and having a look at the place. We knew that the journey was very long and that it would involve a lot of wretchedness, hunger and suffering; but we didn't mind that too much. We were wan with the wretchedness by this time. Our bit of money was getting scarce as well but that didn't worry us either because the way it was out there was every person helping the next—the man that had nothing himself would neither want nor suffer as long as one of his comrades had a bit at all. They used to divide among themselves as if they were brothers and the man that paid back what he borrowed from time to time need have no fear at all.

At this time, we hadn't enough money to get us all up to Klondike. Some of the men that were present weren't too keen on the business anyhow. A couple of older men said that they had often heard stories like this before, but that none of them saw yet the gold that everyone was talking about. Maybe the story was only a newspaperman's exaggeration, an unfounded rumour, that wouldn't be heard of in a couple of months. These thought that they'd stay where they were until the miners came back to the coast with the gold. There were five or six of us in the company, however, that were eager to see this new country and we knew that whoever got there first would get whatever gold was to be had. Since we hadn't enough money between us to get us all moving, it was decided that only three would go—MacCarthy and two others. We drew lots 'long and short', to find out who would go and it fell to Hugh McGinley and Jim Anthony out of my own parish to undertake the journey. Jim had come over from Ireland with me and had been with me in the silver mines and on the whole journey through the mountains after that. I was sorry enough that we were parting now but it was inevitable so I didn't oppose it. I knew he'd send for us as soon as ever he found out if it was worth our while making the same journey.

As soon as the three got all the things they needed—no small amount for there'd be nothing waiting for them in Klondike—off they went, heading for the coast and beyond. The summer would be starting before they would have reached Seattle or Portland and of course there would be no boat going north until then when the thaw would have set in opening up the bays and rivers of Alaska. After they had gone, I went with an old comrade of mine, Owen Cormac, across to Butte where, at this time, they were mining for copper. There was a good price to be had for that mineral but, even so, we were worried that we wouldn't get any work as there were a lot of men hanging around idle. But, just then, there were few of the men that were mining in Montana that I didn't know and we were only a short time in Butte when I came across a man from the North of Ireland that recognized me. He was a foreman in the copper mine and he gave the two of us a start.

The mine was very unhealthy on account of the amount of

sulphur or brimstone that was in the copper but the pay was good and we worked away as well as we were able. We kept saying to ourselves that we would be only a short time there as we were waiting impatiently every day for news from our companions who had gone to Klondike. Well, a full season went by and another one, month succeeded month and every month seemed to us to be as long as a year. In the end, we were actually over a year waiting before they sent for us.

HITCH-HIKING TO THE COAST

By the end of July in 1898, I heard from Jim Anthony that they were working in Klondike, that there was plenty of gold and that they themselves were making a good bit. They had suffered a lot of hardship on the way out, he said, because they had gone through Dyea on the coast of Alaska and, from there, through the mountain passes, through bogs and lakes and rivers until they reached Dawson City from the south. He recommended that we should go to the mouth of the Yukon and get a boat there that would take us right up the river the whole way entering Dawson from the north. This, he thought, was the best and the easiest way from every point of view.

We didn't spend much time discussing the venture. We got ourselves together to go to them and a long journey it was that faced us. Indeed, if we had known when we were leaving Butte what lay before us, I'm telling you we'd have stayed where we were for ever. Our pockets weren't too heavy the day we left but we wouldn't be long in Klondike until every mother's son of us would have them filled with gold. We got together little baskets of food—meat, bread and such—to bring with us. We knew only too well that it would be a long time until we got a bit anywhere else. About ten of us set out from the town of Butte to a place where a goods train passed that would take us a good bit of the way if we managed to jump it.

In America at that time, it wasn't usual for workmen like ourselves to spend much money on travelling when we were able to get a free ride. There were a lot of hoboes who used go from place to place on the trains, 'riding the brake-rods' as we used to call it, or 'riding the blind baggage' (the space between two carriages) or on the roof itself. Riding like this was more than dangerous and many's the man was killed if he loosened his grip for a second, sliding under the wheels or being hit by a water-pipe or something of that kind as he moved along the cat-walk. But we intended to get a right comfortable ride—inside a carriage—if it was at all possible. We slipped into the station in two's and three's, keeping ourselves in hiding as far as we could. It wasn't long until the train came and I'd say it was a mile long if it was an inch. There were eighty coal-wagons and there was only one engine to pull the lot. It couldn't, therefore, go very fast and it had to stop here near Butte to take on more water. The engine left the carriages standing and went around another way to get the water; and that's when we started searching for some way in. In the end, we found a carriage that had a lot of different goods in it and we slipped inside it without any busybody seeing us. We put the lock on the door then and sat back at our ease on big wooden boxes until the train started.

We were on the train through the night until we reached Missoula. This was about a hundred and fifty or two hundred miles from the place we left—towards the north-west. By this time, it was daylight and we couldn't go any further on this train. We said goodbye to it one after another as it was drawing in towards Missoula station. Nobody paid any attention to us throughout this operation or told us that we had no right to be where we were.

We spent the day taking it easy until another train like it would come by us in the evening. It came in good time and we made sure to get into a carriage the same as we had done the day before. Out with us then through the hills—the Bitter-Root Mountains—and on through a big wide countryside where, as far as the eye could see, there was neither house nor hut. 'Prairie' is what that kind of country is called and we went through a couple of hundred miles of it through Idaho and into the state of Washington. There was no beating it for a way of travelling, I thought; and then it happened!

The group that was with me in the carriage was young and lively and lighthearted and had a good share of devilment. When they found themselves away out in the hinterland, what did some of them do but open some of the boxes that they were sitting on to see what was in them. And what, of all things, was in some of them but spirits—not one bottle but a dozen or so in every crate. Three or four of us didn't want to have anything to do with them. We felt that it would be a poor return for a free ride and, particularly as we had jumped the train, that we'd all end up in prison if it was found out. But there was no use talking. We were hungry and thirsty and the temptation was too great.

Well, it was good and it wasn't bad until some of the boys got merry and started to sing. They weren't English songs they sang either but the fine old Gaelic songs that our people way back home used to sing: 'The Red-haired Man's Wife', 'The Bright Autumn Stubble', 'The Summer Will Come', and many more that I don't remember now. And as I'm on the story, I don't think anybody spoke a word of English on that long journey from Butte in Montana. Anyway, the songs were rising bravely from us and wasn't it the worst of luck that one of the train-team came by above us—the guard. He didn't know that there was anybody at all on his train but he heard the noise and the ructions and as quick as you like, he was in on top of us. A flood of abuse poured from him to begin with and then he demanded money from us. Some of us were well satisfied to give him a little but there were others in the company who threatened that it would go hard with anybody who gave him a red cent; what they ordered was that he should get outside as fast as his two legs would carry him. He said no more but got out with a look on his face that would 'stop a wake'.

While we were in Missoula, we collected a good deal of information about the trains and we were told that this one should stop in a particular town where a lot of trains came together. I don't remember the name of the town now but, anyway, we intended to jump off the train as soon as it would start to lose speed. Instead, what happened was that when we came towards this station, the driver accelerated and away with us towards Portland or some other of the towns out south. We knew that if we stayed on it, it would take us a couple of hundred miles out of our way and, as well as that, we'd be arrested as soon as it stopped. We were in a right fix but it seemed to us that it would be a poor thing that we'd give them the satisfaction of throwing us into prison after all we had been through. We resolved that we'd look to leaving the train—and that's what started the talking! It was travelling at a spanking pace by this time but we had no choice—every man of us would have to take a death-jump. We grabbed whatever bags and baggage we had and fired them out through the window. At that, the first man that was ready leaped out after the baggage. One after another followed suit and, thanks be to God, none of us was injured. All that happened was that we were very much separated by the time the last man was out. I'm sure there were almost five miles between the first man who jumped and the last man and all the baggage was strewn along in the same way. We had to gather all that up and each man waited for the next until we all came together again. We were tired and played out by then but, if we were, we were well satisfied that we left only empty space for the man on the train.

When we were all well together, it was the middle of the night and there we were, strangers in unknown country, without the slightest knowledge about the place in which we found ourselves. We thought the best thing we could do was to walk westwards until we came to a house or a dwelling-place where we could ask the way of somebody. Off with us along by the railroad and, after a lengthy walk in the darkness, we reached a place where there was a public house and a couple of other houses. We gave a good loud knock on the door and it wasn't long till the owner stuck his head out of the upper window. He heard us down below talking in Irish—and the first greeting he gave us was to ask, in the purest Irish, what the devil were we up to at that hour of the night. He questioned us as to where we came from and, when he was told, he came down on the spot and let us in. He was as surprised and delighted to meet Irish speakers like this as we were ourselves to meet one, in such a place. But that's the way it was in America then. You'd never know the time or the place when you'd come across an Irishman and, when you did, you'd frequently find that he was from Donegal. This man was one of the O'Beirne's of Glencolumbkille and for a long time, he said, he had been working for the railway company in the town of Tacoma on the coast. He did so well there that he was able to give up the job and buy himself a hotel just where we were. He told us that we were only three or four score miles from Tacoma and that it wasn't far from there to Seattle. He gave us food and drinks generously and plentifully and we spent the rest of the night very much at our ease with him.

The next morning when we'd had a bite to eat, we roamed on again and that day was as hot a one as ever blew out of the sky. I believe that the summers are usually like that on the prairies in the State of Washington that we were crossing. O'Beirne mentioned that the trains didn't stop anywhere around this area—and the reason was because there weren't many people living around since the ground was so burnt and sterile. We walked on, therefore, as briskly as we could, trying to shorten the road to the coast. We were all hot—too much so—and the perspiration was running down us from top to toe. We still had between two and three score miles to slog through over the mountains between us and the sea; and between the sweat and the coal-dust, our clothes were filthy. We felt miserable and could only think how a wash would give us great relief and cool us. We spent the night on the prairie and at last, when the sun was high in the sky the next day, we came by a good-sized stream. We stopped there, took off our clothes, washed them and hung them out on the trees to dry. In the evening, we put them on us clean and we were ready for the road again. Later in the night as it got nice and cool, we pushed off again and kept going throughout the night until we reached the big town of Tacoma by the break of day. We were fagged out entirely by then and we spent the whole day without moving anywhere.

LIFE IN SEATTLE

On foot, we finished the last bit of our journey from Tacoma to Seattle. We were fairly at the end of our tether by the time we got to Seattle. This is a very big town and from it sail most of the vessels that ply to Alaska. About this time—autumn

1898—it looked as if the whole world was on this route. People from the four corners of the world were on the streets of Seattle —and more coming in with each day that passed—miners and other workers like ourselves who had thrown up whatever work they had to go looking for gold in Alaska—servants from the cities, cowboys from Texas, clerks from offices, shopkeepers, outlaws, gamblers and other tricksters that never held in their hands any tool heavier than a spoon.

All the hotels were packed to the doors and there were hundreds around the harbour or in the telegraph offices sending off telegrams appealing for 'grub-stakes'. What that meant was that where a man hadn't enough money to get him up to Klondike, he tried to borrow as much as would keep him going, on condition that he would share whatever gold he found with the one that helped him. Everything a man could want in the Yukon could be bought in and around the harbour—fur coats, snow-shoes, sleeping-bags, mining implements of every kind, tinned food and, above anything you ever saw, special canvas baths! I often thought of that afterwards and how funny it was, when you couldn't let water touch your skin for six months in case it would freeze on you.

People going up north to the mines were advised to take a lot of things with them—a year's food and that, as there'd be nothing to be got on the way or in Klondike itself. We didn't pay much attention to this advice ourselves, thinking that we'd never be at a loss when we had friends out there already—Jim Anthony and Hugh McGinley. But had we known what was in front of us, we wouldn't have made up our minds as easily as all that.

We met plenty of people in Seattle that we had known before—people who had been working in Butte with us previously and who were heading for Klondike the same as everybody else. At the time we met them, our passages were paid on a ship leaving the next day for the mouth of the Yukon but they told us to go another way—the way Jim Anthony went—through Dyea or Skagway and on from there till we reached the head of the Yukon. There we could get a skiff or a coracle from the Indians which would take us down the river as far as Dawson City. If we went this way, our friends told us,

78

we'd reach Klondike quicker than if we went the way we had planned, up the Yukon from the coast. It was getting late in the season now and the danger was that the river would freeze over before we reached our destination. We knew that, but we remembered the advice Jim Anthony gave us and we had heard a lot of stories in Seattle about the dangers of the Chilcoot Pass and about the 'rapids' on the upper part of the Yukon. As well as that, we had got our tickets and we had paid nearly twenty pounds apiece of money we had carefully saved for them. It didn't matter about the tickets, they said, as they had plenty of money and would pay our way by the other route. But there was no use in their talking to us and we resolved to go out by the route we had paid for.

We left Seattle in a large steamer and went up by the coast for a while, turning north-west until we reached the Aleutian Islands when we sailed into the Bering Sea. The voyage was pleasant enough so far and we pitied the poor creatures straining up the Chilcoot Pass; but we were so tightly packed on the boat that it wasn't long until we were singing a different tune. We were heading for the town of St. Michael at the mouth of the Yukon which I believe is up to three thousand miles from Seattle. Anyway, we were thirty-two days on the boat and we were pretty worn out by the time we at last got to St. Michael. By this time, it was near the middle of September.

It was night as we sailed into the port of St. Michael but the sight we saw as the dawn came was both wonderful and beautiful. A hundred boats, from all corners of the earth, were all around us. They were anchored all around the big wide bay as there wasn't room for even half of them along by the quays. There were ships there of every make you could ever see—big ships, small ships, steam-ships, sailing ships, coal-boats, and fishing boats, stylish boats and boats that I wouldn't go to Inishboffin in let alone a couple of thousand miles into the Arctic regions. In those days, however, any ship was good enough as long as it stayed afloat. A number of them, indeed, didn't stay long on the surface and we heard plenty of stories about a lot of them that went to the bottom. We saw ourselves a good deal of wreckage floating on the sea as we came our way up.

Not much of the day passed in the bay of St. Michael before we went ashore in the steamer's dinghies to see what kind of a place it was. And, to tell the truth, you couldn't say that there was much to be seen. Marsh and scrub was all that was there— the kind of landscape called 'tundra' out here, flowers, grass and little plants growing on it at this time of the year but not a tree to be seen between yourself and the mountains at the horizon. There was neither a house nor a barn in the place except for the house owned by the steamship company, and that was only a kind of a big shed where they put their stores. One man was looking after it and that was all we saw of the white man in the whole place. Otherwise, there were only Eskimos and there were hundreds of them on the quays staring at us. We tried to get them to talk to us but we couldn't get anything out of them. They didn't understand us and we didn't understand them and all we could do was laugh at each other.

UP THE YUKON

The boat that was to take us up the Yukon had already left with people who had come to St. Michael before us—Americans and people from a lot of other countries as well. So we had to wait until the boat would come back to take us aboard. We were tired waiting around, particularly as every day that passed meant that there was less chance that we'd reach Dawson before it froze over. However, in three or four days, the boat arrived and we went southwards again towards the mouth of the Yukon—or towards one of its mouths because I believe it has a dozen if it has one.

It was a fairly big boat—the 'Susie'—about four hundred tons with three decks and two funnels. Five hundred of us all told were on her and with that and the amount of baggage, she was drawing four feet of water and wouldn't have floated at all if she had been any lower in the water. She was known as a stern-wheeler from the large paddle-wheel aft that drove her along. She burned a wooden 'rope'—that is to say, a piece of wood about eight feet long, four feet wide and four feet high— every hour and we had to stop every so often at a depot to take on more fuel. Part of the bargain that some of us had struck was that we'd help to get the wood on board and to cut it. This reduced the cost of the voyage for us.

Most of the vessels going up the Yukon at this time were stern-wheelers. The wide paddles in the wheels I mentioned used leave huge waves after them; smoke and sparks flew thickly from the funnels with each 'chug-chug' of the engine as the boat moved slowly up the river. It was a fine sight, I'd say—for anyone that was in no hurry.

All this lower part of the Yukon is entirely tundra— barren sedge-land with neither trees nor rocks to be seen as there are further up. Only mud and dirt are visible by each bank of the river at that time of the year and you wouldn't see a solitary soul—red or white—by the shores for hundreds of miles. We passed a little spot called 'Russian Mission' where the Russian monks used live before Alaska was sold to the Americans. Further ahead, on the same side of the river, there is a little place called Holy Cross where the Jesuits had a mission also. Between these places, a huge lonely mountain was visible for a long time. Dogfish Mountain it is known as—one huge polished rock from summit to foot, very like some of the mountains we knew in Montana.

We left the tundra behind us and came to a place with high mountain on either side of the river—huge sharp peaks rising out of the water with yew and other trees growing thickly down their sides. Some of these rose up to five hundred feet so that you couldn't see much of the surrounding country. There are a great number of islands all along the course of the Yukon and in places the river is divided by them so that now and again, it would be ten miles—and sometimes fifteen—between one branch and another. Some of these branches might be a couple of miles wide—but that is no source of wonder since the Yukon is one of the biggest rivers in America. It is 2,300 miles long and there are other big rivers running into it all along its course.

WONDERS OF THE NORTH

One of the most amazing things we saw on the Yukon was the 'fish-wheel' used by the Indians. This is a great big wheel rather like one of our mill-wheels—a few nets or baskets, tied to it as it turned with the current, catching the fish and flinging them into a trough as the nets reached the top of the wheel. I'd say they catch a lot of salmon with this and I'd believe it the best way for catching them as the salmon there are so well-fed that they'd never bother chasing bait. The fishing is done in the summer; as soon as winter comes with its frost, the Indians move inland and start hunting wild animals—foxes, wolves, beavers and others. The hunters can exchange the skins of these animals with the white folks for other goods.

We were just about in time to see some of the Indians in the camps which they have here and there along the banks of the river. You'd know you were near to one of their camps when you'd get the smell of rotting fish on the wind or hear the terrible howling of the dogs. We heard afterwards that many of these dogs go mad and that the Indians tie them to the trees and let them die of hunger and thirst. Dogs are useless, in their estimation, except in the winter when they could be used to draw the sleds; too many dogs they had for the rest of the year and tradition or superstition didn't allow them kill any of them. It is not killing, apparently, to leave a dog without food or drink as the Indians don't think, as we do, that the dogs have any feelings at all. It seems that such was the case anyway for the barking and the wailing was blood-curdling. It would set your feet shivering to hear it in the middle of the night.

We noticed another strange custom of the Indians on this journey. They had plenty of little cemeteries beside their camps on the banks of the Yukon and it was customary for them to build little houses—about four feet high and decorated with statues and flags—over the graves so that the souls of the dead could live in them. I never saw the inside of one of these little graveyard houses and, indeed, after what one of the boat's crew told me about the food and drink that would be left for the souls of the dead in them, fear wouldn't let me go in. Every Indian in that country liked to have for the souls of his dead relatives a better house than his neighbour and he didn't mind either the time or the money spent on its decoration. I'd say myself that some of these houses for the dead were better and more comfortable than the dirty bothies of those that were alive.

We saw, of course, a lot of animals on this journey up the

Yukon that we had never seen before. I well remember the first moose that I saw. A great black beast it was, but little enough difference between it and an Irish bullock. A lot of us were looking at it as it shambled across the plain from us but someone must have had a special view of it for it wasn't long until a couple of shots rang out and it fell dead on the ground. The captain of the boat flew into a temper. There was no sense at all to it, he said, to kill the beast without rhyme or reason—and as well as that it was against the law; nobody at all had any licence to shoot at animals from a moving boat. That was a lesson for us all. Neither moose nor any other animal was shot at from the boat while we were on it.

Among the other animals we saw were the black bear and the 'grizzly'—a vicious animal that everyone is afraid of—and the caribou. Plenty of caribou crossed our path up the river as they moved southwards for the winter grass. We saw thousands of wild geese flying south also and cranes that sang with the sweetness of harps as they flew south. There were plenty of these birds and many more on the islands and the peaks of the Yukon during the summer and autumn but as soon as the first day of winter arrives, they desert those places and leave the district quiet and lonely after them.

NO CHOICE

We were fifteen days on the boat before we reached Fort Yukon. This was the most northern place that we saw and it's a good bit inside the Arctic Circle. Winter comes very suddenly in that region. By then, it was the beginning of October, the snow had begun to fall and it froze very hard at night time. But the fifteenth day on the river was a very nice quiet day and the captain stopped the boat. He said we were at Fort Yukon, three hundred miles from Klondike, and he had to examine things before he went any further. The boat didn't move at all that lovely day and we didn't know what was wrong. The captain and two of the crew went in a small dinghy up the river. It was a long time before they came back and the captain said that we wouldn't be able to go any further, that the river had fallen drastically since the frost started and that there wasn't enough water to get across the sand-bars. He would have to go back to St. Michael and he would take with him as many as wanted to return—provided they paid their way. Those of us who weren't satisfied with that could stay at Fort Yukon until another boat able to get up the river would come, or we could make our own way back down-river or we could tackle the three hundred miles to Dawson City as well as we could. That was the choice given to us out there in the wasteland with the cold and the wilderness of the north oppressing us.

We were in a right fix then. We had paid our full way to Dawson City and we hadn't enough money left to take us back to America. We impressed this on the captain when he asked us to leave the boat. We demanded a refund of some of the money we had paid since he couldn't take us the whole way, but he didn't pay the slightest attention to us. He threatened that if we didn't leave the boat he would shoot us. There was no use being at him and we had to yield.

There were plenty on the boat that had enough money to pay their way back to St. Michael or to Seattle or to San Francisco itself but there were many workmen like us that hadn't. There was nothing for us to do but to stay where we were and die in the snow or in the forests on the banks of the Yukon or to make our way to Dawson City or to Klondike. We were thrown out into the backwoods—not a thing to be seen but frost and snow, forests and wild animals, without a penny in our pockets or a rag to our backs other than what we stood up in and with no provender except a couple of baskets of food. Well, therefore, we hadn't any second choice; four of us—myself, Conal Allen, Feelim McGinley and Owen Mac-Nally—decided to forge ahead. God alone knew the journey that lay before us—a couple of hundred miles before we'd reach a place where there might be food and drink available. And even then we couldn't be certain with the hungry thousands that might have been just before us.

HIKING IN THE ARCTIC CIRCLE

The dinghies were put out and we were put ashore on the banks of the Yukon. We brought our little bit of baggage with us—fuel, guns, a couple of axes and a few other odds and ends—and we started walking. We couldn't stop anywhere or we would have been quickly dead with the cold. Anyone that stood around would have been frozen straight away. And so, with only God's grace to help us, we tried to move along as fast as ever we could.

We hadn't gone very far before we met a few skiffs coming down the river with three or four men in each. They were all passing us by without anyone taking any notice of us, not even nodding their heads. We thought some group would salute us but devil the notice any of them took of us. They had their own troubles. Some of them were fleeing from Klondike before winter. They had made their pile and had the gold with them. More of them were as cold and miserable as we were and had no interest in looking for gold again until the following summer. But both the rich man and the poor man had the same fear— that there wouldn't be enough food to be had in Klondike to get them through the winter. And so, those who were still alive were going back to civilization before the ice and the hunger killed them. We hadn't any food either and we didn't know what we'd do either where we were or in Klondike—if we ever succeeded in getting there.

We kept walking all this time and at last we came to a place where we saw a little skiff on the bank of the river. When we looked around, we saw three men at the edge of the forest with a fire lighting as if they were getting some food ready for themselves. We went over to them and started talking. We found out that they were from the western states of America like ourselves and, to tell you the truth, they were decent people. They were fleeing south like everyone else and, when we told them why we were walking on, they thought we were out of our minds—going to the place they were leaving without anything with us but our two hands hanging down, one as long as the other. They shared with us the bit of food they had and they said that, if it was any good to us, we were welcome to the little skiff they had with them. They were making for the boat we had left in order to get back to America. We thanked them and said we'd be delighted to have the skiff. We little thought at that time that going up the Yukon was not the same as

85

coming down it and that many a change came over the river at this time of the year.

'KANGAROO' O'KELLY FROM CORK

They went ahead down. We took the skiff and turned upstream, rowing against the current. We had hardly started out before we met people coming downstream in their hundreds. We had plenty of opportunity for talking to them. We had the food the other men left us in the skiff and as soon as we got so hungry that we weren't able to go any further, we turned into the bank for a bite to eat. We couldn't touch any food out on the river because, as soon as we took the oars out of the water, the downstream current swept us a half-mile back as quickly as you could clap your hands.

As we sat on the bank on this occasion, a little skiff with two men in it came down the river. They noticed us lighting a fire and, as they thought we were making downstream also, they came in to talk to us hoping that we would be all down together. When they heard that we were making upstream, they were thunderstruck. They advised and implored us, in God's name, to turn back but there was little use in their talk.

'We've come this far,' I said, 'and we've suffered so much up to this that we're not going to flinch now and let a few little difficulties and a bit of bad weather deter us. God is strong and He has a good Mother.'

We were so headstrong at this stage that we felt it was our bounden duty to keep foraging ahead.

The men had also a little bit of food. We all shared together and sat around the fire eating it. We weren't long chatting away until I noticed one of the men looking at me very sharply. He didn't pretend for a long time but he was listening carefully to all I was saying until at last he asked was I Micky MacGowan. I told him he was right and it gave me the seven wonders to know how he recognized me, seeing that he had never laid eyes on me before. He said that he knew from my conversation that I was the man that some of the people he met in Klondike were talking about. There were plenty of men up that had been with me in the mines in Butte, Montana, and they talked among themselves about the friends they had before they ended up looking for gold in Klondike. This man was so amazed that you'd think I had fallen out of the air at his feet. He gave me a great welcome and, indeed, we both thought of the old saying: The people meet, but the mountains never. We got very friendly there and then as he started to tell me how he had fared himself. He was one of the O'Kelly's from Cork and he had the nickname, as I heard later, of Kangaroo O'Kelly. He told me he had spent nearly two years with my old friends in the remote bleak mountains about sixty miles beyond the place they call Circle City. This is on the Yukon, about two hundred and twenty miles from Dawson and about a hundred miles from Fort Yukon and the boats stopped there on their way up and down. O'Kelly had done very well there, by all accounts, and he was on his way back to the States with his bit of gold. I'll not conceal it, we made a terribly poor mouth to that man and that was the brunt of our conversation.

'Well, Micky,' O'Kelly said to me, 'if you're determined to go ahead, don't be a bit afraid. Keep up your courage and you heart. I'll put in your way enough food to keep yourself and your friends through the winter. I have a cabin in the place I spoke about, sixty miles from Circle, and there's enough flour and tinned meat and anything else you'd want there. There are three sleds there too—one, a brand new one. When you get there, you can take the new one and your friends can have the other two.'

We said goodbye to Con O'Kelly and his friends and started pulling up the Yukon again. The further up we got, the stronger the current got. We weren't able to row any more and one of us had to get out on the shore and tie a rope to the prow. The man that was out there pulled and the other three in the boat used the oars to try to steer it. While the way was clear, we progressed all right but we came on places where there were great trees leaning out across the river that we couldn't get the boat past. We would all have to pile into it then and try to row across to the other side. As soon as we'd reach the strong part of the current, it would swing the boat around as if it were a leaf and we'd loose a good mile of ground before we'd manage to control it. When we'd reach the other side at last, we'd strive as hard as we could to forge ahead until the same thing would happen to us again. We then would have to look to getting across to the other side again.

THE FROZEN RIVER

We were travelling for twelve days like this after leaving Con O'Kelly. Our hearts were broken by then for we didn't know whether we were making any headway at all or not or what would become of us in the end. At last, we caught up one night with a little skiff something like our own. There were two men in it—a young man and a middle-aged man. We found that they were Irish and that they had been on the same boat as ourselves as far as Fort Yukon. After talking things over, we decided that Felim McGinley would go in their skiff so that there would be three men in each of the two skiffs. This was a great help to them because three men could advance better than two. This didn't mean that we could take things easier from then on. The current was as strong as it ever was and it was God himself that saved us from drowning several times. We forged ahead along by the bank of the river and it gave us great heart to have the two boats together like that.

One evening we were at our last gasp and we decided to go ashore and to tie up the boats until morning. We climbed up a high bank that was by the riverside and when we got to the top we saw a little wooden hut that had been built there. There was no roof on it—nothing but the sides and the gables, but we thought it would give us good shelter until morning. We lit a fire and we made a meal out of the little food we had left. We lay down in the old ruin then on one of the frostiest nights that I can ever remember. When we got up in the morning and went back to the boats, the sides of the Yukon were frozen, just like the frozen sea the old people used to tell about in their stories long ago. Winter was with us with a vengeance.

As we made towards the river, I was praying and calling on God that we wouldn't be able to move the skiffs any more. I hoped that they'd be frozen too for my heart was telling me that, if we got them going again, nothing was more certain than that we'd all be lost completely. We were in danger of drowning in any event for we had to walk across the ice to get to them and it wasn't any too strong as yet. If it cracked, we'd have 'got our feet wet'—and it's not in fun I'm telling you that, for it was said of the Yukon that anyone who fell into it was never seen again. In the first place, the cold of the water would petrify him straight away. Then, the river was so full of mud that the body would be covered with it and dragged down by the undercurrent to the bottom as swift as you like. Right enough, the river was getting a bit cleaner and brighter with the coming of winter but that was little comfort to us, the state we were in.

We had to start breaking the ice with our axes to release the boats and also to find out where the water was still running. The Yukon was about two miles wide at this place and there were many currents in it that weren't yet frozen but they, too, were the most dangerous and treacherous. I was praying to myself the whole time with fear but I didn't pretend to the others. As they went out a bit more they saw that they'd never be able to make their way forward and they decided that it would be better for them to get ashore again. My heart jumped for joy when I heard that. I didn't care what happened to me as long as I didn't have to go out on the water again.

We moved around then for a while not knowing where we were nor how far we'd have to go to meet other people. Our biggest worry was that we had hardly any food worth speaking of and, whatever about any hardship that was before us, it would have been pitiful after all we'd been through if it was hunger that killed us in the end. But they say that God's help is nearer than the door. It wasn't too late in the afternoon when we saw large black beasts, something like bullocks, coming towards us at the edge of the river. When they came nearer, we saw they were moose. We still had our guns and we thought that if we succeeded in killing one we wouldn't go hungry whatever else happened to us. We followed them and when we came within range we fired. We hit two of them and chased them until we got some more bullets into them and killed them. We dragged them after us then through the snow back to the cabin by the river where we skinned and prepared them and cut them up. We had nothing to salt them with but you didn't need salt in that country. All you had to do was to chop them into pieces and hang the pieces from the trees. As soon as that would be done, the meat would be frozen stiff and wouldn't need any salt even if left hanging there for six months. Of course, wolves could come and steal it while we slept but we didn't think of that at the time; they didn't come that night anyway. Maybe it wasn't late enough in the winter for them to be ravenous but we learned afterwards that it wasn't safe to leave much out in that country without keeping an eye on it. Anyway, we were heartened by the thought that we wouldn't die of the hunger and that we could forge another little bit ahead now.

CIRCLE CITY

We knew that, by now, we couldn't be far from the little town they called Circle City. There were three of us there, young, strong and courageous and we decided that we'd take some of the meat with us and go searching for that town. We told the three who were older than us that the journey would be too much for them and that they had better stay where the boats were until we returned however early or late that might be. They promised to stay with the boats and to mind our clothes until we got back. We, in our turn, would give them their share of whatever we brought back with us. That was the bargain we made with them before leaving.

We made our farewells and headed off towards Circle City. They were fully satisfied with the bargain and they had enough meat and other food to last them until we got back. By this time, everywhere was frozen over and the bank of the river was as hard as a board. Even during the day, there was little more than a kind of twilight and, as for night-time, it was as dark as a bog-hole. However, we walked fine and briskly through the snow and ice so that we'd get ahead as much as possible before night fell. As the evening closed in, we heard dogs barking a bit ahead of us. This, we guessed, meant that there were people somewhere around and right enough, as night fell, we reached the small town, Circle City. I think it must have been between twenty and thirty miles from where we had left the boats, our clothes and the other men. There wasn't a bit of flour to be had there either for gold or silver because of the great number that were searching for gold in the surrounding countryside. All we could get was canned food but, needless to say, we were delighted to get even that much itself.

We spent the night in one of the large wooden huts that they called hotels there. Most people would think it a very rough place but we had no fault at all to find with it and we were as satisfied there as if we were in the Waldorf Astoria itself. After we had had a rest, we decided that the three of us would go together and try to find the place O'Kelly had told me about—the food and other things we would need to bring with us for the winter. In Circle City, we found out where O'Kelly's cabin was—sixty miles west through Birch Creek in the far hills. We set out for the place.

FROSTBITE

A trail led out from Circle City along by the river but we didn't see it, the snow being very heavy and it being covered. On the first day, the snow was very soft and it was extremely difficult to make any headway through it. We kept on throughout the day but, as night fell and there wasn't a hut or a cabin to be seen along the way, we began to think that something had gone wrong. Up on the top of a mountain we were, not knowing from Adam where we were going. It was an atrociously stormy night with a bitter cut in the wind and the snow falling heavily. But as twilight came, the snow eased and it looked as if it would freeze heavily during the night. We started down the other side of the hill towards the valley beneath and we hadn't gone very far in the pitch darkness until we heard the barking of dogs. In these civilized countries, you often get people complaining about dogs barking in the middle of the night and the same dogs made me angry enough both before and after but I was never so happy in my life to hear them barking as I was that night.

It was so dark now that you couldn't see even to put your finger in your eye but we headed towards the noise of the dogs until we reached the valley at the foot of the hill. There was a large hotel there that used to do good business when the men were living out there in the hills but most of the miners were now trekking to Klondike and the place was almost deserted. We got in, however, and were given something to eat—bread and coffee—and well satisfied we were with this fare. There were plenty of beds, we had our own blankets and we didn't delay much before turning in. But even though I got into bed, I didn't sleep a wink the whole night. I had a queer sensation in my legs from the knees down—something I had never experienced in my life before and I believe it was the long walk through the snow and the cold that brought it on. A lot of people suffered from the same thing in those parts and I often came across it afterwards. The cold would catch you unawares. You were never properly warm even when walking, and if your feet were wet or if you were perspiring, that was where the danger lay. In the twinkling of an eye, you'd freeze as soon as you'd stand and you wouldn't know it until the cramps hit you. If the frost got you while you were sleeping, you were done for. You wouldn't waken up at all.

But I couldn't sleep. I spent the night turning over and over, unable to close an eye not knowing what was wrong with me. The other two lads got up shortly before daybreak so as to start off as soon as they would see what kind of a day it was. But when I tried to rise up out of the bed, I wasn't able to put a foot under me. The others went over to the canteen and left me lying there. They had some breakfast and then came back to get me. Over to the canteen they then carried me but, all the time I was there, not a foot could I put under myself. As God's my judge, I didn't know what was happening to me.

By this time, it was daybreak and we were talking among ourselves as to what it would be best for us to do. The two lads were impatient and they were thinking of going ahead and leaving me there. I told them that it would be an ill deed to leave me behind them when I wasn't able to put my foot on the ground and didn't know from God whether I was going to get better or to die altogether. But there was no use talking to them—they wouldn't listen to me. Off they went. And that shows a thing that I noticed very much in those regions—how selfish even your best friends could get. It was every man there for himself; it was his main objective to save his own life through hardship and hunger; he would grow hard-hearted and callous about his neighbours' troubles. Many's the man got that way and forgot his friends when times got hard. Many's the person that died on the different trails to Klondike and whose bones were left to rot on the side of the road either when he had no companions to help him or when they themselves were too much afraid of death to delay long enough to bury his body.

I never felt so deserted as I did then. I had often been in difficulties before but I had never been without the use of my limbs until then. I had great faith and hope in God at the same time and I never prayed hard to Him in my life that He didn't answer me. People don't know the miracles that God can work until they're in real trouble and what saved me that morning in my affliction was one of God's miracles. I was lying there on the flat of my back, in the sort of bed I had, with nothing around me but snow and ice in the wilderness of the mountains and no face around me that wasn't as cold as the ice itself. My own friends had left me in the lurch and I was sure that all that lay in store for me was to lie there until I died with hunger and thirst—a death without a priest far from home and people. Many is the thought like that that went through my mind as I lay there on my back. To this day, my heart misses a beat when I remember that morning.

I sat up in the bed in some fashion and I prayed to God to come to my aid and, if it was His will, to give me back the use of my limbs so that I could get away from that accursed place. From the moment I said that prayer, I felt that my legs were getting better and after a while I summoned up courage to try to rise on them. Finally, I managed to stand up and I staggered around by the walls a couple of times to begin with. Little by little, I was able to make my way from one end of the house to the other without too much hardship. When I saw how I was, the prayer by which I asked God to help me wasn't half as heartfelt as the one I said to give Him thanks. In time, I got on my clothes and when I felt that I could move around as well as ever, I wasn't long hurrying along the trail after the pair that had deserted me.

TWO KINDS OF BED

A narrow trail twisted this way and that through the snow and I followed it for as long as I could. Before I'd gone a mile, however, the snow came down heavily again and I couldn't see the path. The blizzard was so bad out there that you couldn't lift your head to look one way or the other. As soon as you'd start off walking, you'd have to get your head down and forge ahead—like a bull with its head down for a fight. If you lifted your head you'd as like as not lose your eye-sight with the lash of the snow. I strode ahead purposefully and, though I shouldn't say it, I was better at the walking in those days than my companions and it wasn't long at all until I caught up with them. They were amazed when I swerved out in front of them on the trail and for a minute or two they wouldn't believe that it wasn't my ghost that was there. And, indeed, to tell nothing but the truth, I didn't give them much satisfaction—the two cowards, to go off and leave me as they did.

However, all three of us walked on throughout the day and in the evening we came to a lake that we had to cross. We could have kept to the trail around the side of the lake but out we went across it to take a short cut. As soon as the three of us were out on it, one after the other, the ice started creaking and cracking and it was on the cards that it would break altogether and throw us down in the water so that no human eye would ever see us again. My companions were terrified enough but I had no pity for them and I ploughed my way ahead. They weren't as good soldiers then as they had been when they made off and left me by myself!

As night fell—and it was night nearly all the time now—we came by a forest. We knew we couldn't find our way through it during the night and all we did was to make our way in a bit to one of the thickest parts. We cut down some of the lighter yew branches and lay them on the ground thickly so that the snow was covered. We spread a bit of canvas that we had with us down over the branches and we slept as comfortably as if we lay in a feather bed. We heard afterwards that this kind of a bed is, in fact, known as an 'Alaskan feather bed'. The only danger we were in was that wild animals would come across us; but we thought that the part of the forest we were in was so thick that even those animals couldn't reach us where we lay.

As soon as daylight arrived, we were up and, after eating some bread and meat, we slogged on again. We got along fast enough that day until, as the light was failing, we arrived at another hotel that lay along the trail. There were beds there and cooking facilities and we stayed until morning.

Just like the previous hotel we had been in, this one in no way resembled the swanky hotels there are now. It was a large wooden house built to give shelter and some degree of comfort to those people making their way up to search for gold. There was plenty of firewood around it and it gave good succour. People coming and going to Circle City would go and spend a night there. You had to have your own food and bed-clothes and you would pay for the actual bed and for the night's shelter. And to give the owners their due, they weren't too hard about the money, and if it happened that some unfortunate hadn't a penny, they'd give him shelter free. Our pockets weren't by any means too heavy at this time but we had enough to enable us to pay for the beds.

O'KELLY'S CABIN

Next morning, we set out again. We were thinking that we couldn't be too far now from the place O'Kelly told us about where he had his cabin. As far as we could guess, we had come sixty miles or so and we were half afraid that we might have passed it and left it behind us somewhere. I was swearing to the other two that we couldn't have missed it with the clear directions we had about its location. We were climbing the side of a hill that wasn't too high and before we had finished our argument there we were looking down on the valley below us. Our eyes were caught then by a group of cabins in the valley and we knew we had done well and that we would find the one we were looking for among them.

Down the valley we wended and it wasn't long until we came to the cabin itself. O'Kelly had given us the name of the place and it was 'Dark Rosaleen'. We saw the name in big letters, carved out of the wood over the door. If we had had Spanish wine, we wouldn't have spared it for the same 'Dark Rosaleen', but the times were bad and there was no drink nearer than whatever we could make out of the snow that lay all around us. Happy enough we were, despite that, to see 'Dark Rosaleen.' It was as if she was giving us a great welcome and on her breast we lay that night as comfortable as you please.

There was nothing you could think of that wasn't waiting for us there in O'Kelly's cabin. There was plenty of food and implements of all kinds that we would need. And as O'Kelly had told us that we needn't spare anything once we had got that far, we didn't leave ourselves short. First thing we did, was to light a good fire. There was plenty of good dry wood in the cabin and, as soon as you'd put a match to it, it would blaze up and nearly set the place on fire. Often we hadn't been able to get matches since we started out on our journey but we always carried with us what the old people used—a piece of tinder and flint, and a bit of good dry tow. If we were in difficulty at any time, all we had to do was to rub a couple of those stones together and hold the tow near them. We often lit a fire like that. You have to do a lot of queer things when you're way out in the backwoods.

We spent a good while in the cabin getting ready the baggage we were going to take back with us. But when the morning came, we fell out—and that's where the row started. When O'Kelly met us, he said there were three sleds in the cabin and he told me to take the best one. But when we were getting ready to set out, one of my companions tried to take with him the new sled. But leave it to me; I wouldn't let him. When that didn't succeed, himself and the other lad tried to take away everything that was in the cabin and it was then that I lost my temper with them altogether.

'Isn't it enough for you,' I said, 'that you can take what you need when the man we met was generous enough to offer it to us? Are you not ashamed of yourselves to be breaking and robbing things that you have no need for at all and that you won't be able to carry very far from here anyway?'

They weren't too satisfied with that but they were afraid of me and well enough they might be, for if they made me angry enough I'd have stretched both of them flat on their backs. They were unwilling to try me, however, so they took the old sleds and the flour and a few other things they'd need and off they went and left me by myself. That didn't discourage me at all. My health was good and my limbs were strong; I knew the way and I had plenty of food of all kinds; I was confident now that nothing would happen to me.

I loaded a ten-stone bag of flour on to my sled, a couple of fur-coats, a good axe, a pair of boots and some other necessaries and off I set after the other two. I tied a rope to the sled and pulled it after me as best I could. I was doing well until I came to a mountain that was higher, I'd say, than Errigal. It was hard for a man to try to climb that hill and at the same time pull the amount of baggage that I had with me. But I had no choice in the matter unless I wanted to die before I was half-way up. I knew that if I left the flour behind me death was certain. I'd prefer to die fighting for my life than to die like a coward; so I gathered my courage together and set out for the foot of the mountain. I pulled away until I came to where the mountain got really steep and then I was in a fix. I took hold of the rope that was tied to the sled and went away its full distance from the sled. I sat down on the snow and hauled the sled towards myself. I then left it there, went the length of the rope again, sat down and hauled again. The trail was so slippery that a curlew couldn't keep its feet on it so my only hope was to sit down and dig my heels in well. Even then, I slid down as often as I went ahead.

I went up like that on my backside until I reached the top of the mountain. By the time I was finished, my heart was nearly broken. If there had been two of us together, it wouldn't have been so bad. One man could have got behind the sled and shoved it while the other man pulled on the rope. That's what the pair that left me did and they had no delay at all. But I succeeded myself in the end. When I got to the top, I set out and made good time and soon caught up with the others.

To make a long story short, after three days on the trail, the three of us managed to cover the sixty miles back to Circle City.

ON THE RIVER AGAIN

Between the time we had left the three older men and the time we returned to them, they had got tired of waiting for us. One of them went off on his own, leaving the other two behind him. These were worried about our long absence and indeed I think that they began to be afraid that we had no intention of coming back for them at any stage. A change came in the weather too: the ice started to melt and the great Yukon river opened up again. Down they went to the place where the little skiff lay; they got it out into the river and pulled up towards Circle City. They didn't keep their promise to us. When we got back to Circle after our sixty-mile trek, we were very worn out with tiredness and we spent a night there resting.

Next day, we got a little boat and went down the river towards the place where we had left the older people and the balance of our own gear. But as we were about half-way, who do you think we met but this pair pulling as hard as they could against the current in the better of the two boats. They were so played out that they were hardly making any headway at all. As I said, the current wasn't too strong in by the bank but each time they came to where a tree would jut out in their way, they had to get the axe and fell the tree; if they tried to pull out around it they were in danger of being caught by the full strength of the current and drowned. They had had a fine new axe of ours but they lost it felling one tree and God alone was looking after them from then on.

When we came across them and started to talk to them, my own two companions were raging mad at what the others had done and wouldn't let them get a word in edgeways. But I had a great deal of pity for the poor creatures. As we left them to push ahead to the place they had come from, one of the older men asked me if by any chance I had a little hand-axe with me. I was afraid of my life to say that I had for, if I had opened my mouth, the others would have killed me. I said nothing; but in any event we needed the axe ourselves. They didn't get the axe, so, and we left them to make their way ahead as best they could.

We went on until we got as far as the little cabin where we had left the other three on our departure. We climbed ashore and started to look for the baggage we had left behind us but there wasn't a sight of it anywhere. We never found out what became of it but we surmised that the third man—who had gone off on his own—returned from somewhere and took it away with him. But however it happened, it was gone and we never laid eyes on it from that day to this—or on the man I mentioned for that matter. So there we were left without a stitch of clothes except what was on our backs; and that was a serious matter in that country where death from the piercing cold lay in wait for every man.

The second boat was where we left it. We took it and began the haul up the river again. The two that were with me were in such a rage over the robbery that they were like two madmen. In their rage, they pulled away against the current so hard that you'd think they were going with it and as a result we actually caught up with and passed the two older men before nightfall. We scarcely threw them a word as we passed for none of us was any too pleased at the way we had been treated.

We weren't at all too sure how far we were from Circle City but we saw a little island away across from us on the other side of the Yukon and we made for it. By then, had we any titther of sense or patience, we'd have seen that we were practically looking at the city. But when you're out in the wilderness like that with the perpetual dread of bitter weather and difficulties of all kinds, you're not really able to think properly at all. Anyway, we spent the night sheltering on the island and made off again at the crack of dawn. Circle City was exactly on the other side of the river from us; but the Yukon is so wide and the banks so high that it's easy to go past a town and not notice it. We stuck to the side of the river we were on, looking neither hither nor yon, and there we were all the time turning our backs on Circle City and going completely astray!

We rowed away like that, as hard as we could, for a day or more until we noticed that the countryside through which we were passing was thoroughly unfamiliar. I had been saying to the others that we were heading away from our destination but they were so headstrong that they paid no heed at all to me. In the end, they could see they were wrong and they said they might as well go back. So, when they were satisfied about our situation, they turned the skiff about and with a great deal of trouble we reached the little island we had left a couple of days beforehand. We went up the proper side of the river then and reached Circle City at last. This was our third time in Circle and we were pretty fed up with it by then. We had spent the best part of a fortnight coming and going in this area and Klondike and its gold were as far away as they ever had been.

THE FINNS

From the time my two companions and I had the row at O'Kelly's cabin, we hadn't been all that friendly and I might as well tell the truth—I was waiting myself for the opportunity to be shut of them. But the time hadn't come yet. We were all too dependent on each other where we were and for that reason I thought I'd make a bargain. I had plenty of flour with me and while we halted in Circle City, I offered to give half of it to the other two if they would agree to come back out with me. It was more than a fair offer and they readily agreed.

It was freezing again by now and the boats would be of no further use to us. We had to leave them behind us and start off walking again. McGinley and Allen had a fine canvas windbreaker that they had bought which I coveted as I hadn't got one myself. We got together what baggage we had and waited for daybreak so that we could set out. We didn't delay at all. There was a moon that night that would lift anybody's heart with pleasure. It was more beautiful than any harvest moon I have ever seen in my life. The whole land was covered with snow and ice and there was a kind of an arch or a huge ring of light in the sky like a comb that had brilliant rays coming out of it instead of teeth. Every colour in the rainbow was in each of those rays and it was as bright at midnight as at midday. None of us had a watch or any kind of a timepiece and when we guessed that day was not too far off, we made off. But instead of its being morning as we thought, it was the middle of the night. We found out afterwards that what we had seen was the Aurora Borealis. It's often seen in that part of the world about that time of the year.

A few days beforehand, a big group of Finns left Circle City heading for Dawson and they were the first group to have left from Circle for a long time. We walked throughout the night and the following day and, as evening drew in, it began to snow heavily. When a group of people would be walking through the snow like that, they would have to stay together, one walking after the other. I was out in front this day with the other two following me when the snow got very soft. I said to them that we wouldn't be able to make any headway through the soft snow once night fell and I suggested that they erect the wind-breaker and we'd spend the night under it. 'Maybe,'I said, 'it will freeze during the night and the ground will be hard underfoot tomorrow. We still have to cover nearly two hundred miles and there's no use killing ourselves in this snow.'

Well, we got the wind-breaker up and no sooner was it erected than we heard the sound of bells coming towards us which made us wonder. I said to the others that there must be sleds following after us with dogs drawing them. We listened more carefully then and heard them clearly. We had erected the windbreaker by the side of the trail and shortly after nightfall the sleds came by us. We had a fire down when the men came in and they sat in front of the fire while we got a bit of food ready for them. They were Finns, we found out, but they had a bit of English—as much as we had ourselves—and we managed to make conversation with them well enough. We expected them to spend the night with us but they didn't. They had a team of fine strong dogs and they didn't mind about the snow at all. But we had no dog nor indeed had we the money to buy even one. A dog cost about seven score pounds at that time and if you wanted one you had to go out into the backwoods to get one from the Eskimos or the Indians. A poor man could never spend such an amount of money on a dog so he had to forge ahead as best he could without one.

From the time I had lost the use of my legs on the way up to

O'Kelly's cabin, I was very wary about snow and ice. As the Finns and their dogs took to the road again, I gave some advice to my own companions. 'Now, lads,' I said, 'take off your boots while you have a bit of a fire and dry them and put them back on your feet then. In this way, you'll be much more comfortable when we start off walking again. For my own part, I think we'd be wise not to sleep at all tonight but, when we've eaten and had a bit of a rest, in God's name we should set out immediately and catch up with the dogs before they start off tomorrow. Then when they hit the trail, we can follow them.'

'All right,' they said together.

A couple of hours before daybreak, we took to the road. There was a bitter and vicious wind blowing in our faces down the Yukon and I was out in front of the other two with my head bent into it as usual. I never stopped once until it was bright day and, even with the bad weather we had, made a good deal of ground by then. Throughout the whole time I never turned my head to see if the other two were still there or not. I stopped when I judged there to be enough light but when I looked around there was nobody at all to be seen. I didn't know what on earth had happened to them. I left the sled where I was and went back a bit until I met one of the men, Conal, coming along by himself. I sat on the snow until he came up to me. There was no sight of the other man but he came right enough in the end. We were a long time waiting for him and we weren't too pleased at all at the delay.

I often think of the hardships of that journey and when I do it doesn't surprise me that we were often rough and angry with one another. We hadn't had any proper rest from the time we left Fort Yukon and the steamer. I was in a hurry the whole time for I knew that if we followed the trail that lay in front of us we'd be bound to catch up with the people who had gone before us. When the three of us were together again, we made after them and it wasn't long until we caught up with them where they lay under a wind-breaker. We called on them to get up and take to the road again but one of the men asked us to wait a little while because they hadn't slept a wink since night-fall. I questioned him about what had happened and he said that a big wind arose when they had the canvas up and that there wasn't a bit of it that hadn't been blown down. They had to start off all over again and re-erect it in another place. It was very mysterious: we hadn't been so many miles behind them and no wind like that had hit us! But that's no cause for wonder in those parts.

It was bitterly cold at this time and what, I thought, are we doing standing around here waiting on these people? I spied a little island just across from us and I told my companions that we had better go over and get a little fire going that would keep us warm until the Finns got up.

That was all right; we went over and it wasn't long until we had a fine big fire going strong. The cold was so bad that while the part of us turned to the fire was roasting, the rest of us facing away was freezing. We had to turn ourselves around every couple of minutes like you'd turn a bit of meat on a spit. We were watching the Finns all the time wishing that they'd start getting a move on. But it wasn't too long until they got up and as soon as they started to move we came across to them and followed them and their dogs. We stuck to them like leeches. They were breaking the trail and it made it easier for us to walk after them.

We went along like that for days and we didn't stop except to get a bit of food ready and eat it. We hadn't an idea what day of the week it was, or what month it was for that matter but I think it was about the beginning of December by then and that we had already spent up to two and a half months on the Yukon already.

THE INDIANS' CURE FOR FROSTBITE

One night we were pushing ahead as usual when the snow started falling heavily again. The wind was so penetrating that it was taking us all our time to breathe, even. We knew that we couldn't go much further for, if we did, we wouldn't get very far before we'd have to give up and that would spell the end for us, surely. At the same time, we felt that we couldn't be too far from some kind of a place where people lived. We walked on a bit more and, right enough, we came by a place where coloured people lived. Indians they were, but by then we were so worn-out and fed up that we didn't give a damn if they were devils out of hell itself.

'We'll leave the sleds here,' I said, 'and move up and see what kind of a place they have.'

Up we went.

A couple of days before this, one of Conal's fingers had frozen in the biting cold; since then his hand had been useless and was giving him a good deal of pain; but he was the sort of man that would be at death's door before he'd give in. In we went to the Indians, at all events, and a fine long wide cabin they had, I may say. If there was an overwhelming smell of fish and dogs—and a few other stenches as well—there, we weren't discommoded. They had a fire lighting in the middle of the floor and that was the first time I ever saw a hearth or a fire in such a place. There was a huge fire there and the place was filled with smoke and smuts that failed to find their way out through the chimney hole in the roof. Well, the Indians gave us a hearty welcome. They spoke a kind of pidgin English but when they spoke among themselves, sure a Greek wouldn't understand a word of what they were saying. They were very pleasant, though, and they were as civil to us as if we had been at home among our own neighbours.

As soon as Conal saw the fire, nothing would persuade him to come away from it. But when I thought we had spent enough time there, I told the other two that we ought to be moving along.

'For God's sake,' said Conal, 'stay beside the fire for the night. You've no idea the difference the heat is making to these blasted fingers.'

The other lad wasn't at all willing to wait back. 'We have a long way before us yet,' he said, 'and if we keep delaying like this every second day with the cold getting continually worse, we'll never get there at all.

'Well,' I said, 'I'm sorry for him with his fingers frozen; and since he asked us in God's name, we'll wait for him if these people can give us any room.'

I went and spoke to the Indian that had the most grasp of the English. I asked him what would he charge us to stay by the fire until morning. He made a price and mind you, the sum he asked wasn't all that much—about a shilling a man in that country's money.

'Well,' I said, 'we'll give you that and welcome.'

They gave us little three-legged stools to sit on but they were so low that we preferred to stretch our bones out on the floor. It was an earthen floor and it was covered with little branches from the spruce-trees just like the old houses away at home were strewn with rushes. When we were warmed up and had come-to a bit, I looked the house up and down and saw that there was a fair-sized crowd of people (and a dog or two) under the roof. Some were lying down, others sitting, on rough sack beds or branches on the floor. Soon, they were all fast asleep and we had the house to ourselves. Between then and the middle of the night, we prepared some food for ourselves and we were then well fixed up until morning.

Next day, at the first sign of dawn, we started to move and get on our way but as we prepared to go outside the door, Conal said that his hand was still bad and that he was afraid he wouldn't be able to come with us. It seemed that the heat from the fire had done it more harm than good. We were in a right fix then. We didn't like to leave the poor fellow by himself among all these foreigners while at the same time we wanted to be moving ahead as soon as we could.

I went back to the man that had the English and told him our story. I asked him if he knew of anything that would cure the frozen finger. He said he did. He told us not to move until he returned to us. Off he went and, in a while, came back with an old woman that he brought out of a small room at the head of the house. The old woman wasn't more than four and a half feet high but she was as broad as she was long, not unlike the old women back home. She spoke kindly enough, but we couldn't understand a word out of her mouth. The young man acted as interpreter for us and we managed all right, however. He told us the old woman was his mother.

She looked at our friend's fingers and said that they weren't too bad and that it wouldn't be too hard at all to cure them. I couldn't mention now, for fear of telling you a lie, what were all the things she used in preparing the cure but I know she used snow and something that she took out of a little box. But

what amazed us all was that she chanted some words like a
spell or a charm. Before I had ever left home at all, I had seen
the old women at this—they had a charm for the toothache, a
charm for a sprain and many others—and as soon as I saw this
happening for the frozen fingers, it took me immediately back
home to the old women of my own district. Well, this old woman
said that we'd have to stay over until the next morning if we
wanted to have the cure done properly. At that we didn't want
to leave for, whatever about our hurry, we didn't like to think
our friend would lose his fingers. We said that we'd wait over
and this gave a lot of pleasure to the old lady. The first poultice
wasn't too long on the fingers before she made another one and
this time she put some class of an herb into it. She kept on with
the cure all through the day and by the time night began to
fall Conal was beginning to get some feeling back into his
fingers. He sent the young man to tell the old woman and when
she heard that there was some improvement she came back to
us straight away. She started talking and laughing and we all
had great fun, though it was impossible to know what she was
saying at all.

We offered to pay her then but, if we were to have broken
sticks across her, devil the penny she'd take. All that she was
sorry about was how little she was able to do for us.

MORE COMPANY

We felt in great form for walking when we left the Indian's
house. We had had a good long rest but the thing that pleased
us most was that Conal's fingers were better again. We went
along the trail before us as fast as we could but we had no idea
of how well we were doing or, indeed, of how far we were from
our journey's end. We had heard that there was a hotel along
the trail where we would be within a day's walk or two from
Dawson City. This would be at a place known as Forty-Mile.
It was in Yukon territory, on the Canadian side of the border
between Yukon and Alaska. It had been a great place for gold
a couple of years beforehand but as soon as the news about
Klondike broke, all the miners moved off down south.

On we ploughed for about three or four days and when we

had finally given up any hope of seeing the town, one evening when we hadn't given any thought to it all day, we stumbled across it. We went into the hotel—a large wooden house—and I can tell you that we didn't feel at all lonely all that night. There was a great difference between what we now had and what we had gone through. There were seventy of us gathered there altogether that night. Everyone that had gone that way from the beginning of winter was there before us. Like with ourselves, the boats hadn't managed to bring them all the way up the river. They told us that we'd be in Dawson City by the next day or so and that gave all of us great heart and encouragement. When we got something to eat, we moved around among the people who had got there before us, asking them where they came from and ferreting out information about the place we were making for. Most of them knew as little about it as we did ourselves but there were a few who had been out there before and who had some knowledge of the going. We had no worries now that we were among company. Then the music and the dancing started—the men all dancing together for there were very few women there—and that was the best night's entertainment I, for one, ever had in my life. There were people there from every corner of the globe and there they were in a place where they were neither afraid nor ashamed of hearing their own language. I heard languages spoken that night that I never knew existed. There were plenty of Irishmen there and there was an Irish musician from some part of Connaught that held his own with the best.

We got up as early as we could in the morning and off we went. Almost all our flour was gone by this time and after the hunger and the hardship we had been through so far, we were afraid that, right at the very end, we might be left high and dry. But God is good and He has a good Mother and apparently that fate was not in store for us! The next day we strode on and in the middle of the afternoon, there we were looking at Dawson—on the other side of the river down from us! We felt on the top of the world then for we knew that as soon as we reached that town there would be no danger of us dying from hunger whatever about dying from anything else. We reached Dawson by the evening and it was lucky for us that we did for if we had had to go much further we probably would have died from lack of food. Even though we were tired, we were well satisfied to have come that far and that we had come there safe through all kinds of difficulties and dangers. We had come a long way—about three thousand miles—and had spent a long time on the journey. We had left Seattle in the last week of July and it was within a week of Christmas by the time we got to Dawson. It was five months all told since we had left Butte, Montana.

VI

The Land of Gold

Dawson was something like a country town. Dawson City it was called—and still is for all I know—but it was never a city. Three years before I got there, there wasn't even a single cabin in the place. Anywhere the miners could get supplies, they called it a city—it was the same story with Circle City that I mentioned before. The miners' camps could be scattered as far distant as forty miles away but the 'city' was the headquarters or centre, you might say, of the whole lot. Dawson City was like that and Klondike City which was just opposite on the southern side of Klondike Creek.

Immediately facing the Yukon, on the east side of the river, lay the main street of Dawson—Front Street as it was called. It was a street of wooden houses about three hundred yards long and a few of the houses were two storeys high. A wooden footpath about a foot high ran along in front of the houses in this street but elsewhere there were plenty of cabins and houses with nothing in front of them but the frozen snow. People from every corner of the earth lived in Dawson at this time—the first people to get there on the gold trail. We were told that there were in or about thirty thousand people there in that year 1898 and, naturally, they all had to have shelter of some kind. Hotels were built for them—that or they built cabins for themselves on the banks of the river or on the sides of the hills roundabout. Shops, stores and offices were built, banks, a post-office and a barracks for the police—the 'Mounties'—but above all else pubs were built. Every second house you'd pass was a pub and it's no harm to remark that they were the best-built places in the city. Some of them were open night and day and I'm telling you it was sweet whiskey they sold—it cost a pound a glass. Everything else was proportionately dear. There was a great shortage of foodstuffs in particular due to the fact that no boats were coming in. Flour cost fifteen dollars (about £3) a hundredweight. An apple or a carrot cost a dollar. A meal in one of the cheapest eating-houses cost five dollars and there was no use going into any of the others unless your wallet was stuffed full. One blanket would knock you back 25 dollars and, of course, it goes without saying that water was scarce. It would be brought in from wells in the hills and sold for so much per gallon. But you must remember that when I say that such and such a thing cost so many dollars, I'm not telling you the whole of the story for there was no accepted currency in Dawson at that time, I can say, except gold. At the time I speak of, gold-dust was worth sixteen dollars an ounce and the miners always carried a leather purse or 'Poke' as they called it in which they carried the dust. These 'pokes' were made from moose-skin and served as purses. Wherever goods of one kind or another were sold, there was a delicate weighing scales and it is said that many a publican and waiter and cleaner made a fortune from the dust that was spilt on the counter or on the floor.

I had no gold, needless to say, so that I really had no business in Dawson but at the same time, I wanted to see as much of it as I could. I spent a while wandering around, dropping into the hotels and pubs here and there. I was hoping to meet people I knew—people that had come out before me—but I was by no means expecting the man I finally came across. And, above all other people, who was it but my old friend, Jimmy Anthony—the man I had left Ireland with, who had been with me in Montana and who had sent word for me to come to Klondike the previous summer. Even after giving him the seven greetings, I could hardly believe that it was he who was there. For a moment, I was dumbfounded and there I was standing staring at him before I managed to stammer out a question to ask if it was really himself that was in it. Like most of the other people in that place, he didn't look any too elegant; his face was smeared with grease and ash to protect him from frost, he wore a fur jacket and a huge pair of top-boots. He was breaking his heart laughing at me and, indeed, it was by his hearty laugh that I first recognized him. If I was ever over-joyed to meet someone from home in foreign parts, this was by far the best moment of my life.

Jimmy took me into an eating-house and stood me a good meal and, God knows, I badly needed it at the time. After that, he brought me around all the hotels and pubs that stayed open all night—fine and warm they were inside with a large crowd of men in every one of them. Most of them had a special room at the back for the gamblers, of which there were plenty around the place, as far as I could see. It cost nothing just to go into the room and watch the play. Some game called 'roulette' was what was mostly played. A man at the counter had a large weighing scales and the gamblers threw their 'pokes' on it; they were weighed and put under the counter. The men then got bone or ivory chips which they used while they were playing. Jimmy told me that many a fortune was made and lost at these gambling tables night after night but that, even so, it was seldom that there was any real ugliness. It was easy to understand why. A really tough-looking man sat on a dais where he had a good view of the players; in his hand was a gun at the ready and he had nothing to do all night but keep an eye on those at the table. As well as that, the 'Mounties' were not above a call now and again.

Jimmy brought me along to a large hotel called the Monte Carlo where there was a stage show which was followed by general dancing. Mostly it was girls who sang or danced in the stage-show but I heard a lot about a male singer—an Irishman called Freddy Breen—who sang 'Mother Machree' in such a heartfelt fashion that there wouldn't be a dry eye among the audience. I was told also about the boxing exhibitions that Frank Slavin, the Australian champion, and his sparring partner, Joe Boyle (who made a lot of gold later on), gave and about how Slavin would challenge all who were present to a boxing bout. I'm sorry to say that, although I saw John L. Sullivan fighting with bare fists in the States, I never saw either of these good men at all.

Anybody that wanted to dance could get a partner for one dollar. I need hardly tell you that they were careful not to let a dance go on too long! When one would finish, the man would have to buy a drink for himself and for the girl and that would cost him another dollar. Not one dance did I get out for that night!

Jimmy showed me Sally's cabin and Paradise Alley that night—where the girls of Dawson were 'at home' and where visitors were welcomed at any hour of the twenty-four. At that time the women in Dawson had only one reputation and Jimmy said that, if there was an honest woman in the town, he had never met her. It didn't worry me too much, therefore, that I would be working way out in the backwoods!

As we wandered around that night, Jimmy told me about everything that had happened to him since he had left me in Montana until then and the hardship I had gone through was nothing to what he had suffered. He was in the first rush from the States to Klondike in the summer of 1897. He took the short cut through Chilcoot Pass, up by the great lakes and down to Dawson past the source of the Yukon. He had the most amazing stories about how he and hundreds of others were stranded on the shore of Alaska, all of them trying to save their baggage where the current was running like a river in full flood; stories about the number of dead horses rotting away in the mud; about the like happening at Chilcoot; about the mosquitoes infesting the sedge; about the number of boats that were splintered and the number of persons drowned in the rapids on the Yukon. As I listened to him, I realized that we hadn't done too badly at all.

My old friend was leaving Klondike behind him now; he had gathered a good bit of gold and he was off to America to sell his claim to some company there. By this time, most of the gold-bearing land was staked but a person could always try new areas. Jimmy told me that there was still plenty of gold on the little strip of land he had out by All Gold Creek and that I could go and work it until I found a better place.

'When you get there,' he said, 'take my place and don't be a bit afraid of showing the whole lot of them that you're not afraid of work.'

'I was never afraid,' I said straight back to him, 'of a day's work no matter where I found myself.'

We said goodbye then and as I still didn't feel like sleeping, I meandered around looking at the sights for a bit longer. When I got tired of this at last, I went into some hotel, sat on a chair and it wasn't long until I fell into a deep sleep. I had no fear of doing this for I would have found it easy enough to count my small bit. Nobody, however, paid any attention to me throughout the night and I slept soundly until morning.

LASHINGS OF GOLD

Next day I left Dawson City and made for the place they called Klondike Creek. What we call a rivulet or a stream, they call a creek and Klondike Creek was what the Klondike River was known as—that part that ran westwards to meet the Yukon between Dawson City and Klondike City. I walked east for a couple of miles away from Dawson City until I came to a wooden bridge that had been flung across the Klondike River. From there, I forged ahead for another twenty-five miles to All Gold Creek which I managed to reach before nightfall. That was where the gold-digging went on and I said to myself that, unless I was in for a spell of right bad luck, I was on the pig's back from then on.

There was great work going on in this valley and, indeed, it bore every appearance of it. There were huge piles of gravel and earth stretching as far as the eye could see, men appearing now and again out of the ground like rabbits, smoke coming from some of the holes and a pall of smuts overhanging the whole area. The claims reached from the river up to the hills and everyone's strip was marked with stakes of wood at each corner. Two hundred and fifty feet, by length and breadth, separated the stakes. Everybody, of course, had to be content with whatever bit of land was left by the time he got there.

Each man could only have one claim, and, if he left it, another person could take it. The claims that lay down-river from where gold was first found were those earliest bespoke. It was thought that the gold ran with the current and that you had a better chance of coming across gold below rather than above the 'discovery claim.'

I found Jimmy Doherty's land and started work straight away. A crowd of men from Donegal were working in the same place. The ground was frozen so hard that you couldn't lift a spadeful even if you were chipping away with a pick-axe the live-long day. What you had to do was to light a large bonfire, chip away the area so softened with your pick and your shovel and then light another fire in the same place. When that fire was finished, you'd have to repeat the work and keep on like that until you managed to get down a good bit below the surface.

That's the work I started when I got there and tedious is hardly the word for it! At the same time, we had courage enough to keep it up and be patient for we were hoping to be well-paid for it all when the hole got deep enough. We tried using gunpowder a couple of times to break the ground but it didn't work very well and we had to fall back on the old method that had been proved by the people there long before us. We were working down through the black earth and the gravel like that for five weeks until we were about twenty-five feet down. By that time we struck rock but we struck gold too. But the hard work wasn't over yet. After going down so far, we still had to hack out an area to enable us to work with some ease and that was where the real trouble was! We managed to dig holes at regular intervals around the rock for props, and we then got more than one man working; we also made a little square box rather like a cradle and put a pulley at the mouth of the hole to haul up box-fulls of what we called 'pay-dirt'. We'd leave that lying on the surface throughout the winter. We wouldn't bother about it again until the following summer.

That's the way we worked for a very long time. Not only was the work tedious but it was dangerous and difficult as well. Many was the time, for instance, the holes were filled with water released by the fires. But we had to put up with the tediousness and the hardship. The place we were working was very remote and it was hard to get engines or machinery of any kind out to it. They came there in the end, of course, many years later.

We had to keep working with the bonfires all the time. As the man down the hole excavating the gold would leave in the evening, he had to light a huge fire about four feet high up against the gravel. It had to be broad at the base but narrowing upwards until the last piece of wood was lying in against the rock. Right in the middle, you had to leave a little hole and fill it with dry shavings that would light easily. If that wasn't done, the fire wouldn't catch properly and the work would be held back. The last man up out of the hole would light the shavings and scoot up the ladder of hard birch before he could be burnt by the flames. The fire would burn away until morning and the smoke and sparks and flames would be coming out of hundreds of similar holes in the snow all around us. It was a wonderful sight.

As the fire burned away throughout the night against the rock, it softened the earth and the rock itself and, as it cooled, a lot of stuff would fall to the bottom and keep us busy enough for a good part of the day carting it away. Some of us that were working there were knowledgeable enough about mining and gold and we'd know immediately by just looking at the heap which bit had gold and which had not. Whatever we thought contained it was sent up in the wooden container and we'd shovel away to the bottom of the hole the black earth and anything else that we felt would be of no use to us. When we picked out what fell after the fire and when we sent to the top the gravel and stones that we felt contained gold, we had to light the big fire again—and the day was done: the kind of twilight that we called 'day' in Klondike.

From the gravel, we got fine gold or gold dust but rough gold or nuggets could be found in the cracks between the rocks. Often when I would have finished my day's work, I'd take a candle and go looking in the cracks and many is the time I picked out with the base of the candle-stick a few pieces of gold that I would carry in the palm of my hand—sometimes worth anything up to fifty pounds. But that was nothing besides what other people found. There was plenty of gold in these parts when I was there and the law was in our favour. You could take those pieces to Dawson and have medals hammered from them and, rather than making things difficult, every help was given to you. That wasn't the case in America. In Klondike, you had to pay for a mining licence and you had to pay taxes but the Government of Canada did their best to help any poor man that was trying to make good.

WASHING THE GOLD

We were slaving away there in All Gold Creek throughout the winter waiting for the snow to thaw at the end of spring when the water would run down below the strip we were working. Everyone would have to make a dam just above his own little strip and the dam would be made long before the thaw started at all. In making the dam, you'd have to use a double run of wood; what you did was to put two logs together and fill the space between them with clay and moss. When that froze, it was as water-tight as a bottle.

These dams were built one after another all the way down the river and those lowest down had to bide their time for the water to reach them. The dams were used to wash the gold and separate it from the dirt, and we had big boxes in which to do the actual washing, five feet long and a foot broad and deep, high up on trestles, sloping down into each other. There was a large gate—a sluice gate—on the side of the dam facing the water and one on the other side to let the water through. There was a large block of wood attached to the gate with a chain coming from it so that when the water started to flood, with the rubbish and stones you might expect, we had to haul on the chain and hold it straight away; otherwise the pressure on the sluice gate would get so heavy that we wouldn't be able to pull it back into place.

As the water came to us, in our turn, we washed our gold. All that we had mined would be put into the boxes—soil and sand and stones—and we'd then let the water run in. The dross would be washed away since being the heavier, the gold itself would fall to the bottom of the box. This process lasted a

116

half-an-hour each time and then it would take another half-hour to segregate the gold from the mire left in the box. Then we'd take it to the cabins we were living in and store it in tobacco boxes or suchlike.

As we would finish washing, we'd let the water run down to the man next to us and that process would continue until the man down at the lowest point got, in the end, the use of the water. As you might guess, nobody liked to hold the water back too long. The season was very short and you never knew that the water mightn't stop flowing before the people below you had finished their own work. For this reason, we couldn't sleep day or night while this work was in progress. We had to sit patiently with the gold until it was cleaned properly.

DRYING

The next thing that you had to do with the gold was to 'roast' it. In the summer we did this part of the work when the 'pits were pretty well under water from the thaw and we couldn't do any mining at all. We'd put down a big fire and when it was well reddened, we'd put on it the pan with the gold in it—just as if we were drying oats. We had little instruments somewhat like spoons and we'd turn the gold over and over with them until it was as dry as powder. As soon as it was dry, the next part of the work was to blow the sand and earth off the gold with your mouth and it so happened that this job fell to my lot as often as not. If anyone, at the beginning of my life, had told me that you could get tired shovelling gold, I wouldn't have believed it but, believe me, many is the time I was fed up with it. It was because of this last part of the job that I particularly welcomed a change—such as the drying, perhaps.

There I'd sit at the little table in the cabin with a little tool like a shovel except that it was wide at one end and narrow at the other. I'd fill that with gold, blow the dust away and put the clean dry gold into a little box. I spent two months doing that and nothing else, the first summer I spent in the Klondike. Five pounds a week of it I was collecting at the time—good pay for the days that were in it. I got tired of the work quickly enough and started working underground again. But as soon

as I was a short while down the shaft, my head would start to
spin and I would have to take to my bed for a while. I never
recommended gold-digging to anybody after that!

FUEL SUPPLIES

By the time the gold would be ready, a good bit of the summer
would be gone and we wouldn't have much to do until winter
began again. Not that we were idle. We were always in need
of wood and we'd spend the summer making up a stock for the
year. Although summer is short in those parts, it is fairly hot
while it lasts and the vegetation grows thick and strong. Plenty
of flowers grow in the low-lying areas as well as a lot of wild
fruit—strawberries, raspberries, currants, gooseberries, cran-
berries, blueberries and many others. None of them shoot very
high above the ground and they are all bitter-flavoured. Nor
do the trees grow very high either—only about twenty feet
usually—but there are plenty of varieties—spruce, alder,
willow, birch, poplar and many more that I don't know the
names of.

A large wood stretched for about two miles along the side
of the hill facing us and every tree I have mentioned grew in it.
That's where we cut all our wood. When we'd have a stack cut,
we'd leave it there until winter came and then we'd go up with
the sleds to bring it down. Under each sled, we'd put a long
piece of wood to which we'd tie another with a chain in such
a fashion that it could be used as a steering apparatus. When the
cargo was then loaded, one of us would get on the sled to guide
it down the side of the hill. It would glide over the frozen snow
like a March wind and I can tell you it was a dangerous ride
for if the roots of a tree or anything else stuck out in its path,
the man aboard was bound to be killed. Many is the fright we
got at this work and many is the man was in fact killed at it;
but thank God, nothing ever happened to me when I did it.

FOOD SUPPLIES

We worked there in the same place season after season and
even though the work was heavy and dangerous, we had a

carefree enough time. Fine clean cabins we had and plenty of firing. We had the best of food, too—after we put in the first winter or two, anyhow. When we made a bit of money and got on our feet to some extent, my comrades sent me into Dawson to buy food supplies and other necessaries. Some American trading company had a huge store there in which you could get almost anything in the world you needed. It was a very wealthy firm and it owned a chain of stores here and there along the whole route from the mouth of the Yukon to Klondike. They had boats, too, in which they brought all their supplies up from America and there was always plenty of foodstuffs to be had there at any time. Once a year, I went to the store—in autumn usually—and I had with me a long list of all the stuff I had to buy. I ordered coffee, canned foods including meat, flour, peas and a barrel of whiskey. The whiskey was to help us through the bitterest part of the winter. Many is the man that owes his life to the drop of whiskey when the temperature was '50 below' all around him and he got dispirited and melancholy with the long black night making him lose heart.

I'd leave the order with the store-keeper, pay him and then make for home again. I'd hardly be there myself before the store's dog-sleds would arrive with all that I ordered. The whole supply would be delivered to our door without any extra charge. I would think, though, that the store-keeper did well enough out of it for, as I said before, the food was very dear. The prices didn't worry us for we had money in the shape of gold like turf-dust. We didn't care what we paid for anything so long as it was available and, in time, there was little that you couldn't get there—provided you had the gold. Even the women could be bought there. One rich man said he'd give his own weight in gold to any girl that would marry him in the morning. One lassie said she'd agree to that and the gold was weighed out. But she didn't go through with it after all. The women in Dawson were as crafty as you like—they liked to have their cake and eat it.

It didn't do at all to be in those parts without, above everything else, food; if you didn't lay up sufficient before the beginning of winter, you could go six months without: and life didn't last long up there unless you had plenty of food to eat. The cold was piercing in the winter and it was essential to keep plenty of grub in your stomach. But just to have food wasn't enough. You had to have variety and that was something that our diets didn't have the first years there. We lived almost entirely on canned foods and we never had fresh vegetables. Because of this, a lot of men contracted scurvy: their teeth fell out, they bled and had fierce pains. Many of them died and with my own two eyes, I saw corpses stretched frozen on the tops of cabins—left there in a habit of frost until the thaw came when they would be buried.

Thanks be to God, my comrades and myself were hardy enough and we either avoided the worst illnesses or managed to throw them off rapidly. One thing stood to us, maybe: the bread we ate—a loaf known as 'sourdough'. Those who had been a long time in the area and who knew not only how to make these loaves, but also everything about the place, were called by the same name. It was from the sourdough loaves the name came for these experienced people. A sort of malt— like what you'd use making potheen—went into the sourdough: a mixture of yeast, flour, a little sugar and water. All you had to do was to leave a fistful of the malt in the bottom of the bucket when you had kneaded the dough then you just added the flour and a drop of water each time and you could keep on making loaves till Doomsday in this fashion. I made a lot myself like that. As the name implies, the sourdoughs had a bitter taste but if they had itself, they were wholesome.

The cooking gear we had was what was called the 'Yukon stove'—this was really an oil barrel or suchlike divided in two: you had fire in the front half and a rough oven in the other. It wasn't very swanky-looking but it dispersed the heat very well all around the cabin. This was very important for wherever the heat couldn't reach would freeze and you'd have icicles hanging from the rafters and down the wall. All our pots and table implements and anything else made of metal that was in use had to be kept beside the fire all the time for you couldn't lay a finger on them if you let them freeze. If you let your knife or your tin mug freeze, for example, it would stick to your hand and the skin would come away with it—just like a burn.

A GOOD NIGHT OF STORY-TELLING

We suffered very badly from the cold the first time we got to Klondike but we got used to it and in the end we took no more notice of it than the Eskimos or the Indians. When we'd have our stores laid in from Dawson and plenty of firewood stacked up, there were few people in the world were as happy as we were. There were hundreds of Irishmen there—from every corner of the country from Cork to Donegal. The little cabins we lived in were all more or less together and at night-time, we'd go visiting each other just as if we were at home. Plenty of our own county-men were among them as well as men from further south and from Connaught but our men could hold their own no matter what company they found themselves in. That was well known about them all over the place. If you couldn't stand up for yourself when it became necessary, you'd go under. The Irish got on well enough among themselves but they often fell out with people from other countries. They pulled along very well with the Finns but they were bitter enemies of the Scandinavians—from Norway and Sweden—and I remember that I gave a good beating myself to a Norwegian that called a relative of mine out of his name. What he said was equivalent to insulting my relative's mother and, as that good woman was an aunt of my own, I thought it was only right that I should defend her reputation. That boyo was a quick learner and he didn't need any second lesson from me. To tell you no more than the truth, he was so much afraid of me that he left the district altogether a week later. As I said, we could hold our own in any gathering.

A GOOD NIGHT OF STORY-TELLING

There was a crowd out with us that were good at the music and there were some fine story-tellers among us too. In the long winter nights when darkness fell, we'd go into the cabins, sit by the fires and nearly everybody had his own yarn to spin. We'd all gather in and if there weren't enough seats or stools— which there seldom was—the last comers would sit on the floor. Nobody ever minded that. All the cabins had wooden floors and when they were dry there was hardly a better place to relax. Every man in the company would be smoking and talking and if there weren't too many present the man that owned the cabin would send around a little drop of whiskey. Then the story-telling would start and it was not all about the Land of Gold. Maybe the talk would start off about the market for gold or about the big haul someone would have got about that time or about the latest news from Dawson; but in the twinkling of an eye, the talk would turn to home and you'd soon think that you were in some remote part of Ireland. Someone would start talking about a man he knew back in his home district. He'd tell, maybe, of some fantastic thing he'd have done or that he'd have said. One story would start another and it wouldn't be long till every man would be telling a story of some kind. Then would come tales of the little people, of ghosts, of phantom funerals or fairy wakes, about great Irish warriors right from the time of the Red Branch and the Fianna —every sort of story that you'd hear at home.

I remember well one winter night we were all sitting around in our cabin. There were a lot of us from every part of Ireland. I'd say there would have been about twenty of us there and there wouldn't have been more than four who didn't understand Irish; and it was Irish we were speaking. Myself and my friends found it easy enough to understand the Irish of Connaught but the Irish of the south of Ireland we found it difficult to follow at times. But we got used to it after a while and could follow it as well as anyone. There was a big tall humorous man with us—Jimmy Kelleher from Kerry—and he often told us how he reached Dawson City the first time. Himself and the two men with him had a dog-sled. Food got very short on them and, if you could believe him, they had to cut the tails off the dogs, one after the other, boil and eat them. He told this story to the people in Dawson when they got there in the end. 'Bad enough', said one man to him, 'but if food was all that scarce with you, what did you feed to the dogs?' 'We gave them the soup,' said Kelleher.

As usual, we talked and discussed everything we could think of and someone drew down the subject of a good milch cow. Another man from the south of Ireland was there and, if you were to lop my head off now, I can't remember whether he was from Cork or Kerry but I know he was an O'Sullivan and he was probably from Kerry. He had the best of Irish and he told us that his people at home spoke Irish only. Some man that was with us said, when the talk about the cow started, that he believed that the best milch cow was to be found in Kerry and that part of the country. O'Sullivan said that that was the truth and he began to tell us why the cows were so good there: that it was because the Glas Gaibhleann* gave birth to them all. He had a lot of lore about the Glas Gaibhleann and about its qualities and from the way he talked you'd think they owned it altogether down there in the south.

One of the McGinley family—Hugh McGinley from Magheraroarty—who happened to be with us that night listened carefully to O'Sullivan's story. He was stretched out at his full length on the floor with his hand under his cheek and, as O'Sullivan finished, McGinley got up and urged everybody not to believe a single word of the story. He asserted that the Glas Gaibhleann never left the parish of Cloghaneely at any time and he then began his own tale—and to be honest, he told a story about the Glas Gaibhleann that you might call a story. We had all heard the story as children in Cloghaneely but, if McGinley hadn't started, the Kerry man would have carried the palm, for none of us would have been able to recall our tale. But McGinley did it well. He began by telling about the man who first owned the Glas Gaibhleann, Kenneally of Ballyness: he told of Balor of the Evil Eye in Tory and how he coveted this wonderful cow and how he got it in the end bringing it on to Tory at a place called Portglas to this day. Then he related how it had been prophesied that Balor would never be killed until his own grandson killed him; of how Balor kept his only daughter locked up in the big Tor in the east of the island and of how Kenneally revenged himself for the theft of the Glas Gaibhleann in the end. It seems he managed to get in to Balor's daughter in her prison by dressing up as a young girl. Three sons were born to the daughter and, though Balor tried to drown them all, one survived and it was that grandson who finally drove the red spear through Balor's

*The name of a celebrated cow in folk-lore giving an inexhaustible supply of milk. Sleeping in a field, it gave some of its virtue to the grass and hence to the other cows.

evil eye and killed him. In the meantime, of course, Balor had caught up with Kenneally in Ballyness. He placed Kenneally's head on the stone that can still be seen there and on that stone he beheaded him. From that day to this, both the stone and the whole parish have been known as Cloghaneely which means the stone of Kenneally.

That was the story that Hugh McGinley told out in the Klondike cabin that night but I couldn't—nor did I try—to give it shape or meaning as he did. When O'Sullivan heard this story, he hadn't a word to say. Myself and my comrades from Donegal were so proud of the way McGinley had stood up for the reputation of our county that I was persuaded to pass a drop of whiskey around to all who were present and not to measure it too carefully in Hugh's case. And I didn't!

The spirits didn't stop the story-telling—on the contrary. A little man from Glencolumbkille had been sitting quiet in the corner all the night—a man named Seamus O'Beirne—and when everyone was ready he started on his own accord to tell us a long story that he knew about the Glas Gaibhleann. According to his version, it was God who sent the Glas Gaibhleann down to the poor people. It wasn't long until they became too covetous and they wanted to get from her more milk than they needed. What happened then was that the cow went down into the sea one day and was never seen again.

O'Beirne's story finished the yarning for that night and it was one of the best nights of story-telling that I ever remember. We broke up at last and everyone went to his own cabin and compared the stories and tried to decide which part of Ireland really owned the Glas Gaibhleann. I'm afraid, however, it's a question that has never been satisfactorily settled!

LIFE WITHOUT A PRIEST

There were plenty of pastimes in that remote country for the person who could find them for himself but there were a couple of things that we never got used to at all. What we Irishmen found hardest to bear was the lack of a priest. There was a great priest in Dawson City when I went there first—Father Judge of the Jesuits. He built the first hospital in Dawson and people of all creeds had the greatest respect for him. But I wasn't long in Klondike before we heard that he had died. Dawson was so far away that, in those first years we spent at All Gold Creek, we saw a priest only about once every six months but sometimes a whole year would pass without a priest being able to get to us.

No matter where we were, we tried not to miss Mass if it was at all possible. We often walked ten miles for it, but I doubt if there was a priest within a hundred miles of where we were then. All that changed, though, in our last years there. By then a priest had come to live among us—a Father Magee from somewhere in Tyrone, if my memory is correct. We raised enough money between us to build a small wooden chapel; and we built for the priest a cabin like one of our own. To give all the Catholic miners their due, they never allowed any harm to come to him while we were in those parts. He'd go from cabin to cabin just like one of ourselves and we got to know as much about him as we knew of ourselves. There were people of many another creed there at the same time as us and some of them resented Catholics. But thank God, we were friendly enough with them and, except that they'd seen the poor priest drowned in a bog of water, they'd never lay a finger on him for fear of us. If they did, they'd have got only half the story and well they realized that!

Even when we hadn't got a priest living among us, we never liked to work on Sundays. When we couldn't hear Mass, a crowd of us would get together in one of the cabins and say the Rosary—and say it heartfully. We weren't afraid of others listening to us. Many a time, the cabin would be more than full for the Rosary and those that couldn't get in would go down on their knees outside—which reminded me of home often for I frequently saw people kneeling outside the door of the church in Gortahork in the same way.

ST. PATRICK'S DAY

The Irish always respected St. Patrick's Day even out there in the wilds of the north. Even if his life depended on it, no man would do a stroke of work on that day. There was a fine spirit among all the men and no matter how much it discommoded them, they all behaved the same on that feastday.

I well remember one St. Patrick's morning that we were all out there and we had resolved the previous night that we would do no work next day. We were going to walk about five or six miles down the valley on a sort of a pleasure trip. We knew that there would be a big crowd of people in the village. All the miners were used to relaxing there. As well as those, there were wealthy men there who had made plenty of money and who had men working for them up in the hills. They had nothing to do but to go up now and again and see that the men were working away. And this village in the valley below us was the sort of common recreation place; and that's where we had planned to spend St. Patrick's Day.

As the day dawned, I got up to prepare some water and get the breakfast ready for my comrades when they woke up. In the winter out there, we always had to melt snow in order to get water. There was nothing to it except to get a fire going in the morning and step out for a can of snow to leave on the fire. In no time, there you had water. You had to keep filling the can if you wanted plenty of water. We used that water to wash ourselves, our pots, our clothes and suchlike but we had fresh water as well to use with our food. About two miles away was a source of water which was available every day of the year and despite the frost and snow it never froze. It shot up into the air as if it was being shot from a gun. We'd bring a barrel up and the full of the barrel would last us for a week or thereabouts.

But, as I was saying, I was out at the side of the cabin this St. Patrick's morning filling a can with snow. As I stood there, suddenly I thought I heard pipe-music in the distance. At first I thought it was a dream but in a short while I heard it again. I straightened up then so as to hear it better but as luck had it, didn't the piper stop playing as soon as I was in a position to listen properly. It was some time before he started up again but when he did he seemed to be closer and the music was clearer; and wasn't the tune he was playing 'St. Patrick's Day'! I'd say that by then the piper was three or four miles away up in the hills behind us; there, then, was I, three thousand miles from home but, in the time it would take you to clap your hands, I fancied I was back again among my own people in Cloghaneely. My heart leaped up with so much joy that I was sure it was going to jump out of my breast altogether.

I ran back into the cabin and told my friends what was happening. They came out and when they heard the music, they were so overjoyed that one of them rushed around with the news to all the Irishmen in the neighbouring cabins. They too got up and when they also heard the pipe-music coming towards them they nearly went out of their minds. They went roaring and shouting around the place so much that you could hear the echoes coming back out of the mountains and valleys surrounding us. Everyone waited there until we felt the piper was coming near to us and then we all went out to meet him. Nobody was fully clothed and half of us hadn't eaten at all but our blood was hot and despite the frost none of us felt the cold a bit! When we met him, we carried him shoulder-high for a good part of the way back. He was brought into our cabin and neither food nor drink was spared on him. And it was still early in the day.

When everyone was ready, he tuned his pipes and off we went four abreast after him like soldiers in full marching order. There wasn't an Irish tune that we had ever heard that he didn't play on the way down the valley. Crowds of people from other countries were working away on the side of the hill and they didn't know from Adam what on earth was up with us marching off like that behind the piper. They thought we were off our heads altogether but we made it known to them that it was our very own day—the blessed feast-day of St. Patrick. On we marched until we came to the hotels and we went into the first big one that we met. Without exaggeration, I'd say that there were up to six hundred men there before us—men from all parts of the world. We were thirsty after the march and, though we hadn't a bit of shamrock between us, we thought it no harm to keep up the old custom and to wet it as well as we were able.

We had a couple of drinks each and, as we relaxed, I stood up and asked the piper to tune up his pipes and play us 'St. Patrick's Day' from one end of the house to the other. The word was hardly out of my mouth before he was on his feet.

As I mentioned, there were people from all corners of the earth there and it was daring enough of me to do the like. The piper walked up and down and nobody interfered with him but I noticed that there was one man standing in front of me with a very disgruntled look on his face. He was a tall thin bony man about six feet in height if he was an inch. His face was sallow and he had two wild eyes and a nose with a hook on it like the horn of a slane*. Anyway, as he heard the tune from the piper, he got a glint in his eye like you'd see in the eye of an old codfish thrown into a dark corner some night. He had thick heavy lips also and, as he got agitated, the lower lip would fall just like the lip of a cow trying to pick up the last grain of oats from the bottom of a can. I asked the barman if he knew who it was and he said he was an Orangeman from the North of Ireland.

The piper was playing away and I knew from my man that it wouldn't be too long before he flew off the handle altogether. I was keeping my eye on him and watching the veins in his neck swelling with rage. Finally as the piper passed him once again with the green ribbons hanging down from his pipes, the Orangeman grabbed at the ribbons to try and pull them off the pipes. I saw him and was so seized with anger that, without looking to one side or the other, I went straight over to him and hit him one blow of my fist behind the ear that stretched him out below me on the floor.

There was a bit of an uproar then and I thought something would start; but when the busy-body came to himself, what did he do only get up and walk out the door as quietly as you like, neither blessing nor cursing anyone. That was all and nobody that was present said that I had done a bad thing.

We stayed in the hotel and had a bite of food and, when that was over, one of my companions said that he had to go down to another hotel to see the barman there. He had worked with him for a long time and knew him well. Off he went and he wasn't long gone until we saw him heading back towards us. We expressed surprise at his being back so soon but when he reached us we saw that he was in a bad humour. When we enquired what had happened, he said that the ruffian I had

*A special kind of spade for cutting peat, having a wing on one side only.

hit was in the other hotel and had attacked him as soon as he went in.

There was no need for another word. We all made for the door and headed for the other hotel. We were a fine body of strong young men and our company was increased by five other fine Irishmen that came with us from the hotel we had been in. On down we went with a man named Gallagher from my own parish leading the way. A fine brawny man he was that wouldn't turn the other cheek to any man in that Land of Gold. There were ten steps or so up to the door of the other hotel and on either side of the door were large glass windows. As we reached the top step, we saw the ruffian making for us with some of his own gang that he had collected. Gallagher was in front of our people and, as the man coming down got within striking distance, he lifted his fist and did nothing else to the ruffian but give him a huge clout on the chin that sent him backwards through the window. His friends walked on down without saying a word to us and it was well for them that they did so; for if any man of them had opened his mouth, he'd have got the same treatment. We went ahead in then and some of the gathering there had hold of the man who had gone through the window. He was lying in a welter of his own blood on the floor.

We were sure then that we were all in for bloody murder but it wouldn't have been wise to pretend that. We were so incensed anyway by that time that every man of us would have died for the cause for which we had fought. Indeed, I think St. Patrick would have pardoned such an uproar being created for the sake of his name. But we showed to the people from all those countries that were there that we were faithful to him and that we wouldn't allow anybody, that hated the things we loved, to fling them in our teeth.

When we went into the hotel, we offered the hotel-keeper compensation for his broken window but when he heard the whole story of what had happened, he wouldn't accept a single penny at all. He was as proud of us as a cat would be with its kittens; he gave us food and drink and we spent a most entertaining evening in his place altogether. The man who had been felled went off and followed his own friends. Wherever he went to afterwards, we never laid eyes on himself or any of his friends from that day until we left Klondike.

As night fell, we all gathered ourselves together again and set off up the hill along the way we had come until we reached our own cabins again. We were tired out and it wasn't hard to make our beds that night. The piper spent the night with us and next morning he bade us farewell and went off to the back of the mountain where himself and two friends of his were working. A loyal good-natured Irishman, like thousands of others of his race he left his bones stretched under frost and snow, far from his people, out in the backwoods, where none of his own kith would ever come to say a prayer for his soul. We heard that he had been killed in one of the shafts shortly after he had come to us to keep the Feast of St. Patrick with his music in All Gold Creek.

FED UP WITH GOLD!

We spent three or four years all told working in Klondike and though we were making good money, we were all getting tired of it. We had spent some of the best years of our lives in an unnatural way—much of the time at night-work under the ground while sleeping by day. Often on a lovely summer evening, my heart would be breaking setting off to go a mile and a half underground into a pitch-dark hole leaving behind me a sun that would melt the eye in your head. But I had to do it even though I wasn't satisfied. A man often has to do a lot of things against his will in trying to make a livelihood out there in the wilds. Long years had passed as I slaved away and it was no wonder at all that I was getting well tired of it. Between the Lagan and Scotland and the most remote places in America, I hadn't had much ease from the first day I left home as a child. I had worked hard throughout the whole time; I had gone through deadly dangers and had suffered a great deal of hardship and ill-usage; but, thanks be to God, I had come safe in wind and limb through all.

As we cleaned our gold in the summer of 1901, the little claim we had was just about worked out. The place was getting very dangerous for by then we could hardly light a fire without tons of sand and earth falling down after it. In parts, the ground was so honey-combed up to a bare eighteen inches below the surface that we began to think that the whole lot would collapse on top of us some fine day and that none of us would ever be heard of again. We then decided it would be better to place wood down below. Myself and another man started off and put planks all round the hole we were working in and we made it as safe for ourselves as if we were in a castle. We were satisfied enough then to spend a little time longer underground; but, even so, it was short enough we stayed in the end.

I told before how I had met my old friend Jimmy Anthony in Dawson City on my way up. He went back to the States that time to sell his gold and he never came back into the wilds. He felt he had enough—sufficient to last him for the best part of his life. He had settled down in Seattle and used write to me frequently enough. Ultimately, he asked me and two others from Cloghaneely who were with me to come down to him so that we could all go together and pay a visit home to Ireland, coming back to America again if we felt like it. I told my friends that it would be the height of foolishness for us to leave the place we were in just then—that it would be far better to stay on until we had made a reasonable amount of money. Then, if God left us our health, we could move off homewards and spend the rest of our days in peace there, if we so wished. We wrote and told Jimmy this but he wasn't at all satisfied. He wrote back to us again to persuade us to come down, myself with the other two; but he said that if I still wasn't willing to come, that they too should stay on so as not to leave me on my own.

In the meantime, who did we meet but two men we had come across on the Yukon; they were heading further up the hills where we were working. They had seen a lot of men setting out for the top of the mountain known as the 'Dome' and they guessed something must have been going on up there. This was part of the strange restlessness that sometimes came over the miners and that was known as the 'stampede'. We heard stories about stampedes many a time—about a gold-strike by some river where gold hadn't been found before. There were men in Klondike who would go on every stampede if they thought that the new place was richer than where they were already working. We paid no attention to any adventures of that kind as long as we were getting enough where we were. Maybe that's why we didn't get rich quick! Some of my companions here and there would get this kind of wander-lust now and again but I'd discourage them by reminding them of the old people's advice: 'Wherever the world is heading, head the other way.' But that wasn't for these two boyos. They had got news that gold had been struck on the top of the mountain and, as it was the first time it had been found there, they reckoned that if they got any at all, they'd make their fortune in no time.

These two men met me while the lads I lived with were on their way down to Dawson; and their wheedling and blarney finally made me think that maybe I'd go along this time. They knew I was an old hand at the work and they wanted a know-ledgeable man with them. I said, however, that I could neither say nor do anything until my two comrades got back and that, if they agreed, I'd get moving and be at the top of the mountain almost as quickly as themselves. We parted on that note. My two comrades returned from Dawson that evening. I told them the story—that I was thinking of leaving where I was and following the other two up to the top of the 'Dome'. They lost their tempers with me and said that it was almost impossible to believe that I'd think of giving them the back of my hand after the long time we had been as loyal as brothers to each other. I thought myself too that it would be a poor thing for me to go off like that so I finally put the thought out of my head. But the restlessness and the dissatisfaction with most of our surroundings had taken hold of us all by this time. It wasn't long after that until we decided to make for Seattle and Jimmy Anthony.

A lot of changes had come over the country we're speaking of between the time of our coming and our going. Changes of all kinds there were and we had experienced our share of change ourselves. The pockets that were empty going out were over-spilling coming back. We didn't care what befell us for we knew that we wouldn't be caught out. Places that, three or four years previously, had only narrow trails through the snow, now had the railroad. The railroad didn't reach the wilds we were working in but in 1899 you could get a train from Skagway to

Lake Bennett, and the year after that, it came as far as Whitehorse on the upper Yukon. Machinery was coming out to the
mines too—steam engines to help melt the frozen ground and
to speed up the washing of the gold. Electric light and the
telephone had come to Dawson City. And the biggest change
of all, perhaps—married women were living in the place. As
time went by, the country improved and the life there; and I
don't think anyone would have to spend six months getting up
there like we had to do. But a lot of changes also came nearer
home than that.

BACK TO AMERICA

We worked a little while longer in All Gold Creek until we
cleaned out whatever was worthwhile left in the hole we had
and I can tell you we weren't a bit sorry the last time we came
up out of it. When we had everything tidied up and our little
bit of baggage got together, all three of us said farewell to
Klondike and turned towards America. We took nothing with
us except a few things that were absolutely necessary—a
couple of sleds and a fine dog bought from one of the Indians
for £140. It was dear but we knew it would be of great help to
us on our way. We had plenty of gold, anyhow, to pay for
anything we needed. Off we set down the bank of the Klondike
for Dawson City. It was the beginning of winter—the best
season for travelling provided you had the proper means. The
weather was bitterly cold with heavy snow and frost at night.
But we were heartened by the thought that we were leaving
hardship and discomfort behind us and we took no notice of
the cold or anything else.

It wasn't long until we came by Dawson and the great
Yukon river. One of the stores there was given over to making
a kind of land-boat from sleds such as we had. Under a sort
of skiff, the tradesman would put a sled at the front and another
at the back; a boat-sail then went on high in the middle and
with a bit of wind, off you'd go across the ice like the March
wind. The only difficulty lay in trying to steer the land-
boat.

We were a bit doubtful about this vehicle, the like of which

133

we had never seen on land or sea, at first but when we were told that all the men who had preceded us used them, we thought we might as well try one ourselves. We made a bargain with the tradesman: we gave him the dog that had cost us £140 for one of his vehicles. He was well satisfied with the exchange. The dog was worth a lot in those parts whereas the boat wasn't. We owned the sleds ourselves and all the man had to do was to fit the skiff on to them. He did that and didn't take too long at the job either. He was a skilled man and he had every kind of tool that he was likely to need right to his hand.

When we had everything rightly fixed up, we pushed the boat out on the ice, hoisted the sail and off we went. There was a stiff breeze fine and suitable for us and I can tell you we weren't long leaving fifty miles of the Yukon behind us. The boat had only one fault—it was useless unless you had a fair wind while it was hard to control if you had. Even so, we managed to keep with the wind always so that we weren't smashed against the rocks; and the boat was so light that you could lift it up and carry it across any obstacles.

Southwards down the river, we were coming back to America. It was a different route from the one we had come out by. We moved on down, spending a night here and a night there, until we got back to civilization, with houses and trains and boats and people. Whitehorse was the name of the first town we came to and when we reached there we knew we were practically home and dry. A few Irishmen who had never been in Klondike were there and we took pity on them. We gave them the ice-boat for absolutely nothing and as well as that we gave them the key of the cabin we had left just as Con O'Kelly had given us his key as we set out for those parts years before. We told them that when they got to All Gold Creek, they could go to the cabin and use anything at all that was there. They were rightly thankful to us. We all said goodbye then and, I can tell you, that we were glad it was they who were going up to All Gold Creek rather than us. The 'great wheel of life' moves around always. They were down now, just as we had been seven years before—and I think we actually saw the real bottom of the cycle. But with the help of God, those lads would get their time on top just as it seemed to be our turn then.

We went by train from Whitehorse, through White Pass—where a lot of people perished during the 'rush'—and on to Skagway and down south to Seattle. Jimmy Doherty was there waiting on us and a great welcome altogether he had for us. We settled down in Seattle for a while to relax and you can guess how we needed the rest after all we'd been through. But we had a long way to go before journey's end yet. We were men of substance now; we had changed our bags of gold into dollars and we were where we could spend some of them and get value for our money. We all resolved that we'd see a bit of America and go around at our leisure visiting some of our friends. All four of us went along together and we didn't stop until we had reached California. There were a lot of people from home there that we knew and we stayed a good while amongst them. We were in no hurry to leave the place and all its wonders—and there was plenty to wonder at particularly for a person back after long years in the wilds of the Yukon.

I never laid eyes on a place more beautiful than California. Summer and winter are almost the same there—which is more than could be said about the place we had just left. We dallied a long time there sunning ourselves and talking to our friends and, when we'd had enough of it all we decided to hit out for Chicago. Hundreds of people from our neighbourhood at home were there just then and it's been the same ever since. They all heard that we were in the city and I guess we spent about a month there going round from person to person. Many we met whose people had come there originally in the year of the Famine; others had just come themselves or their people had arrived from time to time after the Famine. One person would bring over the other and at the time I speak of there must have been as many from Cloghaneely over there as there were at home. They were doing well there too, and some of them that had a bit of learning had good posts in the biggest works in the city. But we met many that were sad enough and that would have preferred to live on one meal a day at home than to have owned the whole of Chicago. You'd have to have pity for them with their lives slipping away working hard over there while their hearts were away at home in their own snug little Cloghaneely.

MY BAREFOOT GIRL

When I saw all my friends in Chicago, I resolved that I wouldn't leave the States until I had gone to see the woman with whose household I had lodged in Northampton County. Down we went there and I set out to look for her, and I succeeded in finding the town in which she lived. I went there to the house I had lived in when I first came to America; I knocked on the door and who do you think stuck his head out of the window above me but a negro! I asked him if Mrs. Cannon lived there and he answered, roughly and abruptly, that he had never heard of her. Off I walked down the street to look around before re-joining my comrades and after a short time I dropped into a large restaurant for a cup of coffee. The place was filled with people but I managed to get a place for myself in the end. I wasn't long sitting there till a fine hand-some woman emerged from a room at the head of the dining room and walked down through the place looking from side to side to see that everything was going all right. She moved down until she came near by where I was sitting. She stared me between the two eyes and, as you'd clap your hands, she stopped dead in her tracks in the middle of the floor. She stood still there with her eyes fixed on me; I couldn't think what was wrong with her nor, to tell you the truth, did I recognize her any more than I recognized any other person. And she started breaking her heart laughing!

'Micky,' she said in the purest Irish, 'it looks as if you don't know me.'

'I don't recognize you at all,' I said.

'Don't you remember,' she said, 'the little girl that followed you in her bare feet the day you were leaving for Montana?'

'Anna,' I gasped when I found my tongue, 'I'd know you now.' And we started gossiping about the times that were gone, about relatives and about everything that had happened to each of us since our last meeting. But no matter what we spoke of, we came back again and again to that day many long years before when I had left Northampton County and we laughed heartily about it.

'Do you know, Micky,' said Anna. 'I often thought since then that it was a great pity that I didn't get away with you that time as I wished, barefoot and all as I was, away up to the lands of silver and gold where the big fortunes are?'

'Isn't it weak in the head you are,' I answered her. 'None of those places I was in are fit for a young woman and if you had to go through all the hardship I went through, you'd change your tune. God blessed you when you didn't go on that journey to the Land of Silver and He blessed you twice when you weren't ever in your life within a thousand miles of the Land of Gold.'

VII

A Big House in Cloghaneely

'THE FAIR HILLS OF IRELAND'

Whatever we saw or heard or whoever we met in America, we had now only one wish and that was to get back home to the old country. When we had gone here and there visiting, we made for New York where we'd board the ship to take us home. It wasn't hard to pass the time in New York. You'd think that there must be no one left in Cloghaneely—that they were all by now in New York. The story that we were there in the harbour wasn't long getting around and they were neither cold nor false in seeking us out; but if we had gone to everyone that invited us out, I think we'd have been still visiting.

As the last night came along, all our friends gathered together to say farewell to the four of us that were leaving. There was a large gathering: three cousins of my own and Hugh McGinley's and plenty others between men and women. We celebrated that night—plenty to eat and drink and a lot of music; and, before we parted, there was a good bit of keening too. There were plenty of people in the gathering that were congratulating us on returning home—many that would never see the green land of Ireland again but who spent two-thirds of the day nostalgically recalling to themselves the places where they first saw the light.

On the evening of the next day, we went on board. An Anchor Line ship we had—called the *Ethiopia*. In those days, the boats weren't as big as they are now and this one was only about four thousand tons. They were good boats though—fine sea-going vessels. Our friends accompanied us down to the quays and many of them were heavy-hearted as they said goodbye when we went aboard. Only those sailing were allowed on board but, even so, they didn't move off until the ropes were cast and the horn was blown—a sign that we were about to move. Anyone that wasn't on board by then would be left behind.

Until the pennies are placed on my eyes, I'll never forget the sight as the vessel drew out. The shouting, the roaring and the lamenting of the people on the quays would deafen you and that lasted until the ship was out of sight. As for us, it's no lie to say that we were overjoyed to be turning our backs for a while on the Land of the Snakes and to be facing towards the place where we could draw our breath and take our ease with joy and satisfaction—something we hadn't done since we had left home many long years before. We were nice and comfortable now—unlike the time we set out first. We paid for a first-class passage on that journey home and there was nothing that you felt like that you couldn't get on that 'floating hotel'.

As we left the port, the evening was as beautiful as any you could ever think of. The vessel was as steady as if you were standing on the street of a city. There was nothing much for us to do and we were so tired and played out that we all made for our beds—every person to his own little cabin. Whatever about my companions, I slept soundly until the morning.

I rose early and as I went to wash, I noticed that the boat was rolling a bit. It wasn't only by the uncertainty of my steps that I noticed it either. My head was getting light and I felt that I had two 'apples' in my throat instead of one. I knew I wouldn't breakfast very well but all the same down I went to the dining-room. All told, only half the people that should have been there were present. The bulk of them, it seemed, had my own complaint. It was as heart-scalding as anything I had ever experienced that I wasn't able to eat the meal that was placed before me. It would make your mouth water to see the food that was on that ship but it wasn't pleasure but nausea I suffered as I looked at it. I said to myself that I had seen the day that if such a feast was put down before me, it wouldn't last long. I thought of the cold potatoes and buttermilk of the Lagan and of the bowls of stirabout in Scotland. But isn't everything like that in this uncertain world? We spend our time pinching and scraping and searching for comfort and all kinds of good things and they usually arrive when you're not able to get any good out of them. It was like that with me on this particular occasion. I tell you, I got up as I had sat down —without a bite crossing my lips. Back to my cabin I went and put my head under my arm like a sick hen.

I spent the day as God saw me, dreaming and raving and I suppose I was having a nightmare when I thought the boat was going to the bottom. As it would be settling down on to the sea-bed and I losing my breath, I'd suddenly start up and find myself overjoyed to know that I was still safe and sound. Other times I thought my stomach was being driven out through my back. I'd groan fearfully and I've often wondered that the people in the cabins next to me didn't complain or attack me. But I needn't have worried; most of them were as bad as myself and like myself they didn't know what was going on at all.

That's how I spent forty-eight hours on that serpent of a ship. Thanks be to God, I got some relief then and was able to come out of the cabin. The others were getting better too, and on the third day they were coming to themselves, one after the other like you'd see sheep—not making any comparison—coming together again after a dog had panicked them. Somebody would come on deck now and again like that and all each one had to talk about was how the sea-sickness had seized him. Most of them were starving with the hunger by then; off they went for food and ate every bit they could get.

By then the sea had calmed, the rolling stopped and from then on we had a great time. Everyone moved around as he pleased and there was conversation and companionship such as we hadn't had until then. The weather was glorious. It was neither too hot nor too cold out there on the wide ocean with nothing nearer than a thousand miles to us than the blue sky above. We never noticed the time passing. We had plenty of pastimes. We'd play cards or dance or make music; some of the passengers would read, some just walk around, some drink and others day-dreaming, not knowing what they were doing. And all the time this was going on, the little black busy, sturdy engine was working away, bringing us nearer to our journey's end with every breath it drew.

Saturday night came. We were thinking among ourselves that we must be nearing the Irish coast. One of the stewards came into the cabin while this talk was in progress and somebody put the question to him. 'Tomorrow morning,' he said, 'as the clouds redden, we should be where you can get the fill of your eyes of the green land of Ireland; but I might as well tell you that you won't be given your heads when we get to port, despite that.'

It was true for him. When Sunday dawned, we were in Lough Foyle and anchored in front of Moville. We were overjoyed, and no wonder, as we came on deck when we saw the mountains of our own county within shouting distance. But we weren't allowed to land until Monday. The big ships didn't go into Derry so a little boat came to bring us ashore. Our baggage was brought out and left in charge of a man who was there specially for that purpose. I hadn't much with me for when I was leaving America, I planned to get back there and all I brought with me was what I thought I would need for a short time.

As soon as we put our feet down on the quay at Derry, we saw that there had been big changes since we had left home. Everybody seemed to be in a hurry and they looked to be very busy. We went towards the hotels and the one we went into was fairly full. We ordered a drink of 'The Derry Hag' as the old people used call Watts' whiskey. We sat around and the chat began. There was a man in our company that looked prosperous; he wore a nice black suit, a hard hat and a collar that was almost touching the tips of his ears. He got very friendly and one of us treated him. He saw that we were on our way home from America and it wasn't long until he started to tell us about the changes that had come over the country since we had left it.

'You don't have to walk to Cloghaneely this time,' he said,

'as you and your fathers had to. The train goes now and you'll be able to take it as far as Cashelnagor.'

'It's good to hear that,' we all said together.

'And what's the reason for this sudden change?' I asked the gentleman.

'I'll tell you that,' he said, 'if you have time to listen to my story. A Board was set up called the Congested Districts Board and some years ago a man named Balfour visited your parts. He enquired about the condition of the people and when he had done that, he conferred with people in authority about schemes to help the poor districts that stretch from here westwards to the sea. As a result of that, the railway between Letterkenny and Burtonport was started.'

'It couldn't be that this work took very long,' said one of my friends.

'It didn't,' said the gentleman, 'and that's where the workers did themselves damage. They were so enthusiastic at the work that it only took two years to build the railway. Gangs of them all worked together and they tore hills away and filled in little valleys and it wasn't long until there was silence again all over the place. If they had had any sense, they could have made the work last much longer. And the pay they were getting wasn't even all that good—they were working from dawn to dusk for a half-crown a day.'

'What way did they bring the railway?' asked Hugh McGinley.

'They brought it out the very cheapest way for themselves,' said the gentleman, 'and they'll rue it for more than today. They built it as straight as they could over hills and dales and it doesn't go within miles of any village from here to Burtonport. If they had built it along the coast, as they should have done, the land would have been dear but instead they bought the cheaper land and built it around by the foot of the hills. Of course, from the tourists' point of view, it goes through some of the loveliest countryside in Ireland.'

'The fishermen of the Rosses have benefited by it,' said a man from Burtonport who was in our company.

'You could say that,' said the Derryman, 'and it will do this town good too. It has done so already. There's a man in this town that has made a small fortune out of clocks since the railway started—a man named Faller. He began making clocks and selling them for a pound each and there isn't a house between here and Arranmore that hasn't a clock now.'

'They can sell the cocks,' said Hugh McGinley, 'a lot of changes have come about in the world since Columbkille cursed Kilcock and since he prophesied that no cock would ever crow there again.'

'Changes there are,' said the Derryman, 'and the people down by the sea where you live can be thankful to this new Board for many of them. They've done well for the fishing all around the coast; roads and bridges were built; grants were given to poor people to help them to build new houses; they're helping home industries and the weavers are very busy now making bawneen. There are twenty ways in which they're trying to help the people, late and all as it is. But better late than never. And above all, the people in your county are lucky that you have that fine churchman, Dr. O'Donnell, as Bishop to guide them. I'd say that there is no other man in Ireland, cleric or layman, that the government authority respects so much; not that he's anyway pliable for he's a first-rate Irishman. It will be a long day before the people of Tyrconnell* forget him for they owe much to him.'

We heard plenty more about how Ireland fared and we listened carefully to every word of it. We spent all that day, and the night, very pleasantly in Derry. We were delighted to have our feet on Irish ground again and it wasn't like the old days when we passed through Derry on our way home. We were well supplied and we didn't mind spending. And signs on it, we didn't spare the money.

Next morning, we left Derry. We were longing to see the old home itself. The train wasn't in too much of a hurry, even if it was new. If you were a good walker, I'd say that there were many stretches where you'd have had no trouble keeping abreast of it. There were times when you'd have the urge to leave it altogether—like one man who went to America long ago and who grew impatient with the sailing boat he was on. He said he'd be better off walking—that he'd get there quicker.

*The old name of Donegal.

Once when one of the two men who were in charge of the train came into our compartment, I asked if it wasn't possible to make it go a bit quicker. He didn't answer but sat down for a minute at my side.

'Did you ever hear of Columbkille's prophecy?' he asked.

'I did, surely,' I said.

'Well,' he said, 'it was about the Black Pig's race: that the day would come when the black pig would race from Derry Bay to Burtonport. This is the black pig of the prophecy—and you never saw a pig going fast!'

He got up then and went off roaring with laughter.

In the end we got to the station at Cashelnagor and I don't suppose anyone ever got off a train feeling as good as I did then. My heart was broken with all the travelling: it was a long way from All Gold Creek to Cashelnagor. I'd have so much of my fill of trains and boats that I preferred to walk the last five miles home rather than look for any kind of transport. Of course, the only thing available was a horse and car. We got to Gortakork on foot and in the hotel there we took it easy for a while and had some food and drink. The door was as open and as welcoming there that day as it ever had been.

THE OLD HOMESTEAD

Many's the change that came over the village between the time I left and the time I returned. A lot of the old people of the neighbourhood had gone to their eternal rest and a new genera-tion had grown up. The district was settling down again after the end of the Land War; and the clouds of oppression and suffering were lightening somewhat. Movements had been founded that were giving the people heart again. Schools were going up and parents were paying more attention to the acquisition of some kind of learning. The Gaelic League had been established and political movements that were inspiring the people and giving them new courage were operating. And even the conditions and pay of the men who worked in Scotland were improving.

One place hadn't changed much since I had left—my own village. All my people were still in the land of the living and as they belonged to the older generation, they hadn't changed a bit. That didn't upset me in any way: I had seen enough of the modern times in America; and it was like a healing balm to find myself under the old rafters again.

In those days, it was always a great occasion when a Yankee came to the village. All the neighbours would gather in and unless the man was a complete miser, he'd provide a bit of a feast for them. The person that didn't do that, would be a figure of fun all round the parish and his life wouldn't be worth living. I knew all this so I didn't arrive empty-handed. In came the neighbours sure enough and between music and chat, the next day was well dawning before I got to stretch myself out on my bed. And some were still there when I woke up and they put in a good bit of the next night for me too!

ANOTHER TWIST IN MY FATE

I spent a long time wandering around the district afterwards, between two minds whether to go back to America or to stay where I was. I think I was unable to make up my mind for about six months. A couple of the lads who had returned with me were trying to persuade me to go back with them but, somehow, when I got the taste of home, I didn't like to think of leaving again. But more than in any place else I had been, I had got little ease over there; and seeing that I brought enough back with me to keep me going for a good part of my life, I didn't care for America and I often said to myself that if I ever had a family, I'd never let one of them go there. I'd rather have seen them gathering rags!

Life is certainly very queer with its many twists and turns. While I was turning over in my mind the idea of going back to America, a couple of things happened that settled the whole thing for me despite myself.

There was a well-known shop-keeper in Meenlaragh at that time called Hugh Dickson—Hudie Owen he was known by in the neighbourhood—as nice a man as ever walked, and now and again whenever I'd feel like a chat or a drink I'd drop in on him. He had four daughters working in the house and in the shop and pub and after a while, the same thing happened to me that happened to many another man—I fell in love. Maire—the second daughter—was my choice. From then on it was a woman rather than the States I was interested in; but I had to get the nest ready and, unlike the wren's nest, it took time to prepare.

THE BIG HOUSE

Shortly after I came home, Johnston's house over at Cashel near Gortahork was put up for sale. Johnston was a landlord though not in a very big way and as long as he lived at Cashel, the Johnstons never had enough land. When their little bit of money was all gone, they had to start borrowing. The big landlord in our area was Alport who lived at Ballyconnell near Falcarragh, and right wealthy he was too. Whenever Johnston was feeling the pinch, he used to borrow from Alport—a hundred pounds this year, a hundred and fifty the next year and so on year after year. In the latter end, Alport got tired of all this and when Johnston next came looking for accommodation, he refused it. This so enraged Johnston's wife that she went straight to the parish priest, Father Hugh McFadden, and offered him a bit of the land if he wanted to buy it. Father McFadden bought a good bit of it and the parish built him a fine presbytery there—which broke Alport's heart, for he was a sworn enemy of the Catholics always. The Johnstons left the place altogether then. They had another place over in England and their children were at school there. The place came in due course to a relation of theirs, Sir John Nicholas Dick. He lived in Surrey and it was from him I bought the place for a thousand pounds—which was a lot of money in the early days of the century.

All the neighbours were overjoyed when they heard that I'd given the wheel another spin and many was the wonderful story that the old people told me about Cashel. There were three or four people on either side of the river in particular and there was no lore about the place that they hadn't on the tip of their tongues. One of the things I wondered about most was the strange arch over the main gate on the drive leading to the house. It wasn't long until I heard all about it.

A couple of hundred years ago, the sea threw up a huge sea-serpent on the strand at Magheraroarty. It was incredibly large and people were saying that it was swallowing a boat that caused its death. When Johnston heard about it, he went down with some of his men; he skinned it and brought a big lump of it back with him on his car. He put the jaws and one of the ribs stretching from post to post over the main gate. The rib is fifteen feet long and any passer-by can see it there to this day. Some of the smaller ribs, Johnston put over gaps elsewhere around the house, but there is only a couple of them left now.

These old people I mentioned were simple, contented, credulous people and they wouldn't be at all satisfied if they thought you had any disrespect for their traditional stories; though some of them were hard enough to swallow without difficulty. They would also have it that there was a cave under the ground near the house and they said that well back in that cave there was a crock of gold hidden with a snake entwined around it and a sleeping warrior in full array guarding the hoard. They were so certain of this that they did their level best to get me digging for the store. They'd tell, too, how priests used be put to death under the very roof during the persecution and how there was an instrument of torture something like the 'collar of Morann'* that would be put around the priests' necks to cut their heads off. They also said that there was a Johnston in the place during the 1798 Rising and that, when there was a great sea-battle out beyond Tory between the French and the English, he gathered all the silver in the house and buried it under a tree in the garden. It seemed that when he did this, it was the night of the full moon and they said that it was by the moon he marked the hiding place. The mark was this: the full moon shining on the centre chimney and the berry bush east of the house. A fine mark, indeed! But however fine it was, it didn't help me at all to come across any bit of that wealth.

I bought Johnston's place at all events—earth, stones and bones. There were about a hundred and fifty acres there, excluding the priests' bit, with barns and fine cow-sheds. The dwelling house was poor—a long thatched house, two stories

*The collar of Morann, the brehon, which grew tight around his neck whenever he pronounced an unjust judgment.

high. As I said, the Johnstons had left the place years before and though Sir John Dick had it, he never paid any attention to it and it was almost a ruin. My troubles were only beginning then. I'd have to look to building a new house, buy horses, cattle and farm implements. So I thought that before I undertook all that, it would be best to take Maire Bawn unto myself according to the law of the land as they say—which I did in spring 1902.

I succeeded in doing everything I set out to do but I couldn't have managed without the help of my brother Jimmy whom I brought over from Pollanaranny and who spent the rest of his life with me. Maire did well for me too and it was a great blessing to have such a good woman of the house. Many is the burden she lightened for me, though she had plenty to do herself with eleven children to bear and rear.

SOLDIERS AND SCHOLARS

When we were properly settled down and the house finished and furnished, we heard that an Irish College was going to be established in Cloghaneely. Many famous scholars—clerical and lay—got together and the college known as the College of Ulster was opened in 1906. It was in a dwelling house at Ardsbeg in the beginning but the numbers of students grew so fast that they had to start thinking of erecting new premises. At that time, my friend and cousin Thomas Cannon, God rest him, had bought the priest's house in Glenna and he gave them a bit of land for the college for nothing. Roger Casement was there at the time and being very interested in the Irish language, he gave them a fine subscription to get the work going.

From the time the College of Ulster was founded, many is the famous and enthusiastic Gael that spent days and nights in my house. There'd be a whole book in my litany if I was to name them all but it's proud I'll be till the day I die that, on my own floor, I shook hands with that noble soldier, Patrick Pearse. I well recall that autumn evening in 1906 when I was leaving the house to go down to my friend Sean McDonnell, to buy a scythe. This, by the way, was the same Sean that was a policeman in Meenadrain when I was working as a herd—the man that used to bring the tea out to me by the side of the road. He was married then to a woman from these parts and he had a fine shop down by the bridge. When I was ready to walk out the door, I saw this man standing looking at the serpent's rib over the gate. He walked over towards the house then. I knew nothing whatever about him at the time but after some talk, he told me who he was. As he left, I walked down the main road with him, step by step, and when we got to the top of the road, I thought he'd go down to the hotel but it so happened that he too was going to McDonnell's place. We moved on and at the bridge he stopped to bid me goodbye. I shook his hand and after saying farewell to him, I said: 'You'll come back to us next year?'

He was silent for a minute as he looked down the road.

'I'll come back again,' he said, 'if it's the will of God.'

I never saw him again.

Many another famous man I met and many of them stayed with me here at Cashel. Among them were Roger Casement, that I mentioned before, Eoin MacNeill,* Eamonn O'Toole,* Robert MacAllister* (who left no stone or hill unexamined), Seamus Delargy,* the folklore expert, and our own Seamus Sharkey* who came to us year after year. I had a great respect for everyone of them just as I had for all the scholars that came to us from Germany, Sweden, Norway and other countries in Europe. Most of them only stayed a short while and so I didn't get to know them as well as I got to know some of our own people. But there's one man I'll never forget—Dr. Heinrich Wagner, a young Swiss scholar who came here without much of our local Irish at all. He spoke Irish like they speak it in the south of Ireland but for a couple of days or so, he might as well have been talking German to men. The young people understood him all right but it wasn't like that with me.

God leave him his health, he wasn't with us very long until he knew our Irish and when he left us he was more fluent than we were ourselves. My heart warmed very much to Henry (as we used call him). He was just like one of ourselves here and a nicer or more understanding person never slept under my roof. He put his heart and his mind into his work and as soon as you

*Well-known Irish scholars, historians and archaelogists.

had a word out of your mouth he had it written down exactly as you'd say it. You'd think he was writing music. He was heavy on two things: sleep and cigarettes. When he'd go off to his bedroom and lie down, he'd start snoring and it would remind you of nothing other than distant thunder. He was so heavy a smoker that the room in which he'd be working would be so full of smoke that you'd think he was burning seaweed. He had another trait that I liked—from the day he came until the day he left, there was never a crooked or contrary word came from his lips. I don't suppose I'll ever see him again, but whatever country he'll be in, he'll still be a fine Irish-lover and scholar.

I little thought in my day out there in the wilds of the Yukon and only rough ignorant men all around me, that the day would come when I'd be talking to the great scholars of Ireland and Europe and that they'd have great respect for my conversation and for the Irish language spoken in Cloghaneely. Many of those I spoke of are dead, God rest them, but it's very inspiring for me, an old man with one foot in the grave, that there's none of those that are going but are leaving a fine new generation after them. I won't live to see the result of all their work and enthusiasm. Great work has been done in my time and I hope and pray that the coming generations will go from strength to strength. I pray God that none of them will ever suffer the hardship that I and the people who lived with me suffered as we were whirled around on the Great Wheel of Life.